THE BETHUNE BLUEPRINT

The Bethune Blueprint

Transforming Your Life Using the Lessons of Dr. Mary McLeod Bethune

DR. EVELYN BETHUNE

John-Mark McLeod

Contents

Dedication   vii

Forward   ix

Introduction   1

1   Build Your House on a Solid Foundation   6

2   Courageous Convictions: Channeling Inner Strength   14

3   Empowering Education: Elevating Through Knowledge   29

4   Resilient Resonance: Rising Above Strife   46

5   Sisterhood and Solidarity: Building Supportive Networks   61

6   Political Prowess: Advocating for Equality   74

7   The Power of Faith, Vision, and Education   90

8   Radiant Resurgence: Reclaiming Your Power   104

9   Visionary Vibrance: Imagining a Brighter Future   116

10 Mastering Mindfulness: Cultivating Inner Peace   131

11 Bountiful Blessings: Cultivating Gratitude and Generosity   144

12 Legacy of Love: Embodying the Spirit of Dr. Mary McLeod
Bethune   157

Relevant To The Cultural Development Of Students And Teachers   173

Support A Movie   177

About The Author   183

Dedicated to

My Family - The McLeod Bethune Tribe
BlackCEO Team
Trevor, Spaulding, Tiffany, and the dynamic crew of gifted
and giving Black people who truly believe in the
advancement of Black People
Pastor Nathan M. Mugala and my church family -
Allen Chapel AME Church - Daytona Beach

Forward

Greetings Architects of Change!

As we stand at the crossroads of history, the pages of "The Bethune Blueprint: Transforming Your Life Using the Lessons From Dr. Mary McLeod Bethune" beckon us to leap into a reservoir of wisdom that is both timeless and profoundly relevant. In a world where the cacophony of daily life often drowns out the whispers of our own potential, this book stands as a guiding light—a beacon that illuminates the transformative path that each one of us is capable of walking.

This remarkable blueprint is not just a collection of stories from a bygone era; it's a roadmap for empowerment, resilience, and leadership that transcends generations. Dr. Mary McLeod Bethune, a luminary whose legacy continues to radiate, becomes our guide. Within these pages, her life story unfolds, a narrative woven with threads of determination, courage, and unwavering vision. As we immerse ourselves in her journey, we recognize the echoes of our own desires, aspirations, and yearnings for change.

History is not merely a chronicle of the past; it's a tapestry that shapes our present and informs our future. The Bethune Blueprint underscores the profound power of knowing our history, drawing from it the lessons that inform our actions today. Dr. Bethune's life becomes a mirror reflecting the transformative potential that lies within every individual. The wisdom she imparts through her journey becomes a source of encouragement, a reservoir of strength that fortifies our resolve to overcome challenges and push the boundaries of what we thought possible.

I commend the author of this masterpiece, Dr. Evelyn Bethune, for her dedication to carrying forward her grandmother's legacy. Dr. Evelyn Bethune's commitment serves as an example of leadership in its purest form—a leadership rooted in preserving and disseminating the essence of empowerment. The torch she carries lights the way for us all, reminding us of our duty to uplift one another, to empower those who come after us, and to etch our mark on the annals of history.

In a world that often rushes forward, where progress is measured in the speed of technological advancement, we find solace in the timeless lessons imparted by Dr. Mary McLeod Bethune's life. The Blueprint offers a chance to pause, reflect, and cultivate the qualities that underpin transformative leadership. From courageously pursuing convictions to nurturing relationships and embracing self-care, each chapter weaves together a mosaic of principles that can guide us on our path to leadership.

The Blueprint reminds us that leadership is not confined to the boardrooms and stages; it's a practice that begins within, manifesting in our actions and the ripples we create. Dr. Mary McLeod Bethune's unwavering advocacy for education resonates deeply, as we realize that knowledge is the cornerstone of empowerment. Through education, we acquire the tools to dismantle barriers, to challenge norms, and to cultivate the change we envision.

Furthermore, Dr. Bethune's legacy of sisterhood and solidarity becomes a testament to the power of unity. In a world that thrives on division, her example stands as a clarion call to lift each other up, amplify voices, and create a tapestry of inter-connectedness that is stronger than any individual thread. The Blueprint beckons us to foster compassionate connections, to mentor and be mentored, and to realize that our strength multiplies when we stand together.

At the heart of this transformative journey lies the recognition that leadership is an embodiment of authenticity. Dr. Mary McLeod Bethune's commitment to her principles, her unyielding spirit in the face of adversity, and her unapologetic embrace of her uniqueness—all these elements illustrate the essence of authentic leadership. The Blueprint encourages us to align our actions with our intentions, to cultivate our unique gifts, and to empower others through our unwavering authenticity.

As you embark on the journey through "The Bethune Blueprint," remember that its lessons are not confined to these pages; they are a call to action, an invitation to lead with purpose and authenticity. The stories within these chapters resonate not just with Dr. Bethune's journey but with the journey of each of us, a reminder that transformative leadership is within our grasp.

In conclusion, let me urge you to embrace the transformative potential that lies within you. Let "The Bethune Blueprint" become your guide, your companion, and your source of empowerment. As you navigate its pages, remember that leadership is not a destination but a continuous journey—a journey that requires resilience, authenticity, and unwavering commitment. Dr. Mary McLeod Bethune's legacy lives on through you, as you step into the role of a transformative leader in your own right.

Now, armed with the wisdom of the past, go out there and be great.

With utmost respect,
Trevor Otts Founder & CEO
BlackCEO

Dr. Mary McLeod Bethune - Looking back over my years...
DrEvelyn

Introduction

The Bethune Blueprint

Unveiling Your Path to Empowerment

In the vast tapestry of time, there are figures whose stories echo through the ages, their voices carrying the essence of courage, resilience, and unyielding determination. Dr. Mary McLeod Bethune stands as one of these luminaries, her legacy a guiding light that continues to illuminate the path of empowerment, resonating profoundly with the aspirations and dreams of Black women in America. Within the pages of the Bethune Blueprint lies not just a collection of chapters, but a transformative odyssey inviting you to embark on a journey of self-discovery, empowerment, and growth.

As you venture into the heart of this narrative, you will find yourself woven into the fabric of Dr. Mary McLeod Bethune's extraordinary life. Her story serves as a compass, pointing toward the untapped reservoirs of your own potential, the richness of your uniqueness, and the profound purpose that can be found in authenticity.

In the opening chapter, we delve into the roots that nurtured Dr. Bethune's indomitable spirit, mirroring the struggles faced by many. Born into a world that did not easily yield to her dreams, she emerged from humble beginnings with an unwavering determination to transform adversity into opportunity. It's a lesson that resonates deeply, reminding us all that our origins need not define our destination; rather, they provide the fertile ground from which our strength and resilience can flourish.

The story continues with the chapter that reveals the courageous convictions that birthed the Daytona Educational and Industrial Training School—a beacon of hope akin to modern educational endeavors. This chapter reveals the challenges faced and the unwavering faith harnessed, inspiring us to summon our inner strength, carve our own path, and stand firm in our beliefs, understanding that within us lies the power to shape our realities.

The merging of institutions that Dr. Bethune championed is emblematic of her fervent belief in education's transformative power. As we explore this merger, we uncover the significance of knowledge as the bedrock of empowerment. It urges us to embrace the journey of lifelong learning, invest in personal growth, and either find or become a mentor, underscoring that knowledge is not merely a tool, but a dynamic force for change.

Through her fight against racial discrimination and injustice, Dr. Bethune's story echoes the contemporary voices confronting systemic inequalities. Her spirit inspires us to rise above barriers with courage and engage empathetically with the world. This chapter compels us to cultivate inner strength, confront adversity with unwavering fortitude, and join hands in creating a better future for all.

Dr. Bethune's legacy extends to the bonds she forged through the National Council of Negro Women, reminiscent of modern efforts to create supportive networks. The chapter dedicated to sisterhood and solidarity invites us to form lasting connections, nurture relationships, and uplift one another. It emphasizes the strength that lies in unity and the transformation that occurs when compassion becomes our guiding light.

The pages turn, revealing Dr. Bethune's ascent to advisory realms—mirroring the journeys of contemporary women who wield influence. This chapter offers insight into the art of advocacy, navigating intricate systems, and catalyzing tangible change. It reminds us all that our voices hold power, our actions can sculpt policies, and our advocacy can shape destinies, urging us to embrace the opportunity to become agents of justice.

As we journey deeper, we discover the chapters unveiling Dr. Bethune's philosophy and teachings, guiding us toward a life infused with authenticity and purpose. The essence of her message echoes the power of embracing our core values, aligning actions with intentions, and nurturing spiritual resilience. It invites us to understand that the path we walk is ours to define, and our unique purpose has the potential to inspire generations.

In the face of setbacks, Dr. Bethune's resilience becomes a beacon of hope and strength. Her ability to transform adversity into triumph resonates deeply, reminding us that setbacks are not the end, but new beginnings. This chapter urges us to overcome obstacles, rediscover our determination, and embrace our inherent worth, demonstrating that our challenges can serve as stepping stones to resounding victories.

Through chapters that evoke visionary optimism, mindfulness, gratitude, and generosity, Dr. Bethune's story weaves together a tapestry of empowerment. Her acts of kindness and philanthropy resonate as a testament to the boundless capacity for compassion within us all. As you read, you will discover that gratitude is a gift we give ourselves, generosity multiplies our impact, and compassionate connections thread our lives with significance.

As the final chapter approaches, the legacy of Dr. Bethune stands tall—an enduring testament to the potency of empowerment. This chapter invites you to absorb her teachings, honor her service, and embrace the responsibility of carrying her legacy forward. Dr. Mary McLeod Bethune becomes not just a historical figure, but a guiding light, inviting you to sculpt your destiny with authenticity, resilience, and boundless love.

As you immerse yourself in the Bethune Blueprint, remember that empowerment is not just a destination—it's an ongoing journey. The chapters within these pages offer insights, lessons, and inspiration that are not limited to history but speak directly to your life, your dreams, and your aspirations. Let the legacy of Dr. Mary McLeod Bethune ignite a fire of empowerment within you, and let this blueprint be your guide toward a life lived with purpose, authenticity, and unyielding determination.

With Love and Power
The Dr. MaryMcLeod Bethune Family Legacy, Inc.
The MMB Project

Education is one of the Keys To Freedom
*Created by Dr. Evelyn Bethune using Midjourney: The facial image is
the merging of Dr. Mary McLeod Bethune, Dr. Evelyn Bethune and
Mrs. Elizabeth Bethune (Mother of Evelyn)*

Chapter 1

Build Your House on a Solid Foundation

Mary Jane McLeod, a young girl with a fierce determination to rise above her circumstances, was born into a world of challenges and hardships. Born of parents who were enslaved in rural South Carolina in 1875, Mary grew up in a family with 17 children. Her brothers and sisters worked long hours in the cotton fields, to feed their large family and also work the 5 acres of land that her parents owned. Owning their land gave them better chances than most to have a better life than was offered to their people after enslavement. Many had nothing and depended on the fairness of their past owners which always put them on the short end of the stick. Yes, freedom had come but for many not much had changed. Despite these trying circumstances, young Mary was different from her siblings. As the first child in her family born free, she had dreams of a better life and a strong desire to overcome her obstacles. Her parents raised their children with a strong faith in God and a clear understanding that they were better than their circumstances.

One pivotal day, Mary accompanied her mother, Patsy, to work. While there, she found herself playing with the white children on the plantation. Curious and eager, Mary picked up a book, only for one of the white children to snatch it away from her, exclaiming, "Put that book down nigger! You can't read!" In that moment, Mary experienced a powerful realization: she needed to learn to read and write if she was to change her life and create a better future for herself and her family.

Driven by her newfound determination, Mary began to pray for an opportunity to learn. And as fate would have it, her prayers were answered. A Protestant missionary visited the plantation one day, announcing the opening of a school for the children of the plantation workers. Seeing their daughter's resolve, Mary's parents chose her to attend the school. This marked the beginning of her education. As she learned, she taught others in her community, including her parents, to read and write.

Mary's relentless pursuit of education eventually led her to attend Barber-Scotia Seminary (now College) in North Carolina and Moody Bible Institute in Chicago. Through her unwavering dedication, she went on to become a trailblazing educator, political leader, and civil rights activist.

Mary's story resonates deeply with influential women today, such as Michelle Obama. Like Mary, Michelle has dedicated herself to the cause of education and empowering young girls. Both women recognized the power of education to transform lives, and they harnessed that power to inspire and uplift those around them.

In this chapter, we will explore the following points:

· Born to Build: Embracing Your Roots

· Education as Empowerment: Unlocking Potential
· From Humble Beginnings: Navigating Struggles
· Lessons in Leadership: Rising Above Challenges

Born to Build: Embracing Your Roots

Mary McLeod Bethune's journey to education began as she stepped into the schoolhouse, embracing the opportunity her parents and the Protestant missionary had given her. With each day, her literacy skills grew stronger, and she became increasingly aware of her own potential. Mary was not content with simply improving her own circumstances; she felt a sense of responsibility to uplift her community as well. As she learned to read and write, she eagerly shared her newfound knowledge with others in her community, including her own family.

Just as Mary found strength in embracing her roots and recognizing the power of education, modern Black women can draw inspiration from her story. Mary's journey demonstrates the importance of acknowledging and celebrating one's own background, even when society tries to dismiss or devalue it. By understanding and appreciating our roots, we can forge our own paths and contribute to the collective success of our communities.

In a world that often marginalizes the experiences of Black women, connecting with trailblazers like Mary McLeod Bethune can be a transformative experience. It is essential to remember that the struggles and triumphs of those who came before us are an integral part of our own stories. By reflecting on the resilience and determination of women like Mary, we can find the strength to build on their achievements and create a brighter future for ourselves and those around us.

Education as Empowerment: Unlocking Potential

The power of education to transform lives and unlock potential is undeniable. For Mary McLeod Bethune, education was the key to breaking free from the limitations that society placed on her as a Black woman in the late 19th century. Through her pursuit of education, Mary not only improved her own life but also the lives of countless others.

Mary's story serves as a powerful reminder of the importance of education as a means of empowerment. In a world where access to education is still not equal for all, it is essential to advocate for the right to learn and grow. By investing in our own education and that of others, we can continue to break down barriers and create opportunities for future generations of Black women.

Michelle Obama's focus on education and empowering young girls is a prime example of the continued importance of education in the 21st century. By sharing her own story and advocating for greater access to education for girls worldwide, Michelle carries on the legacy of women like Mary McLeod Bethune.

From Humble Beginnings: Navigating Struggles

Mary McLeod Bethune's journey from a humble background to becoming a trailblazing educator, political leader, and civil rights activist was filled with struggles and obstacles. Her unwavering determination and resilience allowed her to overcome these challenges, ultimately making a lasting impact on countless lives.

Mary's story teaches us that it is possible to rise above the circumstances we are born into and create meaningful change. Her life serves as an example of how the power of perseverance and self-belief can lead to greatness, even in the face of adversity. Navigating struggles and overcoming obstacles is a part of life, but it is how we choose to confront these challenges that ultimately define us. When faced with difficulties, we can draw inspiration from Mary's life and remind ourselves that growth often comes from discomfort and adversity. By embracing our struggles and learning from them, we can move closer to achieving our goals and realizing our full potential.

Lessons in Leadership: Rising Above Challenges

As a leader, Mary McLeod Bethune faced numerous challenges, from discrimination to financial constraints. Yet, she never allowed these obstacles to deter her from her mission to uplift and empower her community. Mary's leadership style was characterized by her ability to rise above challenges and stay true to her vision. One of the most significant lessons we can learn from Mary's life is the importance of resilience and determination in the face of adversity. Her ability to remain steadfast in her beliefs and persevere despite setbacks is a testament to her strength of character and serves as an inspiration for modern Black women.

By embracing the lessons in leadership from Mary McLeod Bethune's life, we can develop our own leadership skills and learn to rise above challenges in our personal and professional lives. Her story is a powerful reminder that we can overcome obstacles and leave a lasting impact on the world.

Your TO-DO List

We have explored the life and lessons of Dr. Mary McLeod Bethune, a trailblazing Black woman whose determination, resilience, and leadership continue to inspire generations of individuals seeking to create a better future for themselves and their communities. From embracing her roots to the transformative power of education, Mary's story serves as a blueprint for personal growth and greatness.

As we reflect on the lessons from Mary's life, it is essential to remember that we each have the power to make a difference in our own lives and in the lives of others. By following in her footsteps and applying the lessons learned from her journey, we can unlock our own potential and achieve greatness in our personal and professional lives.

Action Steps:

1. Embrace your roots: Take the time to learn about and appreciate your own heritage and the contributions of those who came before you.
2. Invest in education: Pursue personal growth through continuous learning and use your knowledge to empower yourself and others.
3. Develop resilience: Learn from your struggles and setbacks, and use them as opportunities for growth and self-improvement.
4. Cultivate leadership skills: Embody Mary's lessons in leadership by rising above challenges, staying true to your vision, and leaving a lasting impact on your community
5. Advocate for change: Use your voice and influence to create positive change in the world and inspire others to do the same.

By applying these action steps to our own lives, we can continue the legacy of Dr. Mary McLeod Bethune and empower ourselves and our communities to reach new heights.

7 Affirmations for Chapter 1

1. "Just as Dr. Bethune rose above challenges, I am equipped and destined to overcome any obstacles in my path to greatness."
2. "My roots, heritage, and the trailblazers before me empower my journey towards success and fulfillment."
3. "Every day, I commit to lifelong learning and growth, understanding that knowledge is the key to unlocking my potential."
4. "I am resilient, drawing strength from adversity, and using challenges as stepping stones towards my purpose."
5. "Inspired by Dr. Bethune, I lead with grace, determination, and vision, impacting those around me positively."
6. "I harness my influence to advocate for positive change, ensuring that my voice creates ripples of transformation in my community and beyond."
7. "Empowered by the lessons of Dr. Mary McLeod Bethune, I am on a journey of self-discovery, purpose, and greatness."

Wisdom of the Ages
Dr. Evelyn Bethune - Creator

Chapter 2

Courageous Convictions: Channeling Inner Strength

In the early 20th century, a young black woman, Mary McLeod Bethune, was confronted with the stark reality of systemic racism and deprivation. Education for African Americans was scarce, substandard, and heavily segregated. Her community in Daytona, Florida, was bereft of learning opportunities for black children, many of whom were consigned to lives of labor from a tender age. Mary, the child of former slaves and herself a beneficiary of limited education, recognized this significant problem. She was determined to remedy the situation and forged a path where there seemed to be none.

With only $1.50 in her pocket, Mary Jane McLeod Bethune dared to dream big. She envisaged a school where black children could access quality education, a place where they could nourish their minds and, ultimately, uplift their lives.

The opposition she faced was immense. Prejudice, financial constraints, and the rampant racial discrimination of the era threatened to quash her audacious vision. However, she was not to be deterred.

Similar to the circumstances that many women have found themselves in when they decide to follow their dreams, and their mission, Mary Jane McLeod Bethune was alone with her young son, Albert, venturing into an unknown arena. Yet her faith never faltered. She trusted that God would open doors for her and Albert so she pressed on.

With unwavering faith and relentless determination, Dr. Bethune set about solving the problem. She began by renting a small cottage, her faith convincing her that the meager sum she possessed was enough to embark on this noble mission. Equipped with some used crates for desks and a small supply of pencils and paper, Dr. Bethune opened her school, offering education to a handful of black children. She was their teacher, their principal, their mentor, and their biggest champion.

What began as a modest initiative rapidly gained traction. Dr. Bethune's school started to bloom, attracting more and more students. The community began to rally around her, extending support in various forms. Her school's reputation spread, turning into a beacon of hope for African-American education in Daytona.

Fast forward to the present, and we witness the same un-yielding spirit in Oprah Winfrey, a figurehead of resilience and empowerment. Her Leadership Academy for Girls in South Africa mirrors Dr. Bethune's early efforts in Daytona. Amidst local resistance and doubts about the feasibility of the project, Oprah persisted. Today, the academy stands as a testament to her commitment to education and the empowerment of girls in a country plagued by gender-based violence and inequality. Mary McLeod Bethune did not have the resources that were available to Oprah, yet she did not give up. Bethune-Cookman University is a visual of her unyielding faith in God. That faith fueled her relentless pursuit to educate Black people despite the obstacles.

Dr. Bethune's story and Oprah's endeavors serve as stirring reminders of the transformative power of a single individual's conviction. From her solitary school in Daytona to Oprah's Leadership Academy in South Africa, the ripple effect of courageous convictions is palpable.

In this chapter, we will delve deeper into the journey of courageous conviction. Specifically, we will explore the following:

1. Visionary Ventures: Crafting Your Mission - We will study how to create a clear vision, using Dr. Bethune's founding of her school as a guiding example.
2. Fearless Faith: Overcoming Doubt - We will analyze how to maintain an unflinching faith in the face of doubt and adversity, inspired by the faith that fueled Dr. Bethune's determination.
3. Unwavering Will: Staying True to Your Path - We will discuss staying committed to your path despite challenges and detours, drawing parallels from Dr. Bethune's persistence in keeping her school afloat amidst all odds.
4. Transformative Tenacity: Persevering Through Adversity - We will examine how to exhibit tenacity in adverse circumstances, taking cues from Dr. Bethune's unfaltering spirit to keep going in the face of difficulties.

Let's embark on this journey together, drawing wisdom from the past and courage from the present, and let us channel our inner strength to foster a future filled with promise and opportunity.

Visionary Ventures: Crafting Your Mission

Every significant venture begins as a small seed, a spark, an idea fueled by a vision. For Mary McLeod Bethune, that seed was her fervent belief in the transformative power of education. Her vision was crystal clear: she desired to cultivate an environment where African-American children could receive quality education. She recognized the necessity of this venture not just as a quest for knowledge, but as a potent instrument for liberation and empowerment.

Crafting a mission, such as the one Dr. Bethune embarked upon, requires more than an inspiring idea; it demands a deep-seated passion, an inflexible commitment, and a willingness to traverse a challenging journey. However, as her example illuminates, when a vision pulsates in your heart, it instills an indomitable spirit. Dr. Bethune proved capable of overcoming even the most formidable obstacles.

In crafting your mission, the first step is to discern the 'why' of your endeavor. The 'why' is the primal force, the core motivation, the profound conviction that propels you forward. Dr. Bethune's 'why' was unequivocal: she perceived education as a vital catalyst that could elevate the status of her community, providing them with opportunities for growth and prosperity.

Once the 'why' is identified, it serves as a guiding light, illuminating your path even amid challenges and uncertainties. The subsequent step is setting clear, attainable, and quantifiable goals. Dr. Bethune's goal was explicit: to establish an environment conducive to learning for black children. To accomplish this, she delineated several objectives such as securing a location for the school and procuring necessary teaching materials.

However, having a vision and setting goals are not enough on their own. The most crucial part lies in the detailed planning and diligent execution of the implementation process. With meager resources and an unfaltering spirit, Dr. Bethune initiated her school in a humble cottage. Despite the modest setup, she was determined to provide her students with quality education. She supplemented the standard curriculum with lessons on vital life skills such as cooking and sewing, thereby ensuring her students were not only academically proficient but also equipped to be self-reliant.

Dr. Bethune's approach to visionary ventures resonates powerfully even in contemporary scenarios. Consider the example of Oprah Winfrey's Leadership Academy for Girls in South Africa. Like Dr. Bethune, Oprah began her endeavor with a clear vision: to render world-class education accessible to girls in South Africa. She identified her 'why' in her belief that empowering girls through education is the cornerstone of sustainable development and societal transformation. Following in her footsteps, Oprah set attainable goals and meticulously planned the implementation process.

Crafting your mission is an odyssey that requires strategic thinking, but more than that, it is a testament to your dedication to the vision, a manifestation of your commitment to your 'why,' and a tangible demonstration of your desire to effect change, no matter how grand or subtle that might be.

As we progress to the next section, consider these questions: What is your 'why'? What is the vision that fuels your passion, and how do you plan to actualize it? The path ahead might be strewn with obstacles, but as Dr. Mary McLeod Bethune showed us, a compelling vision can illuminate the darkest corners, leading us toward our goal despite daunting odds.

Fearless Faith: Overcoming Doubt

A vital element in every journey is the ability to navigate the tempestuous seas of doubt. Dr. Bethune's determination to establish a school for black children was undoubtedly a daunting challenge, riddled with numerous obstacles. Yet, her fearless faith served as her compass, leading her through uncertainty and doubt.

Faith, as it's often understood, is a conviction, a belief in something unseen, unproven, or unknown. For Madame Bethune, faith was an active, living entity. It wasn't just a belief in the possibility of what could be, but a force that propelled her to act, despite the daunting odds. It served as her armor, shielding her from the sharp arrows of skepticism and derision. It was her fuel, providing the energy to persevere in the face of adversity.

Overcoming doubt requires the courage to face it head-on. Doubt, after all, is not always a negative force. In fact, when approached constructively, it can serve as a tool for critical thinking and reassessment. However, doubt becomes a hindrance when it paralyzes, instills fear, and halts progress. Dr. Bethune encountered her fair share of doubt, both internally and from her surroundings. Yet, her unshakeable faith in her vision allowed her to rise above this debilitating uncertainty.

Facing doubt also necessitates drawing strength from within and around. Dr. Bethune's faith in God was her bedrock. She leaned heavily on her spiritual beliefs for support, comfort, and guidance. Similarly, she derived strength from her community, the parents of her students, and even the unlikely support from gamblers and "honky tonk" owners. These sources of strength fortified her faith and enabled her to stand tall amidst the challenges.

Just as importantly, overcoming doubt means continuing to take steps forward, even when they are small and uncertain. Her approach to securing a new location for her school exemplifies this. The only available place was a landfill dubbed "Hell's Hole." Despite the seemingly insurmountable challenge, she saw potential where others saw despair. Guided by her faith, she negotiated a deal and took the crucial step towards expanding her school. In each step, regardless of its size, her faith was apparent.

Similarly, today's influential women such as Oprah Winfrey demonstrate the power of fearless faith in overcoming doubt. Oprah faced numerous obstacles in establishing her Leadership Academy in South Africa, from bureaucratic hurdles to cultural differences. Yet, she pushed through the doubt and uncertainty with unwavering faith in her vision.

Overcoming doubt, therefore, is not about completely eliminating it. Instead, it's about acknowledging its presence, using it as a tool for introspection, and allowing your faith to guide your actions. Mary's story underscores that fearless faith is not just a state of mind; it's a state of action. It's about taking one step after another, no matter how challenging the journey might seem. This relentless pursuit of the vision, in spite of the doubters and naysayers, is the true mark of fearless faith.

As we venture into the next section, remember this: Faith and doubt are not opposites; they are companions on this journey. One prompts questioning and introspection, while the other fuels the courage to continue. As you face your own doubts, may you find, just like Dr. Bethune and Oprah Winfrey, the fearless faith within you to persevere and overcome.

Unwavering Will: Staying True to Your Path

Remaining committed to your path despite the odds is a testament to the strength of your will. For Mary, this journey was marked by a firm, unwavering will that anchored her in the tumultuous tides of opposition and adversity. Regardless of the setbacks, her resolve to provide education to African-American children was unyielding.

Mary McLeod Bethune's story exemplifies the notion that the will to persevere is fueled by an unshakeable belief in one's mission. The continued growth of her school, despite its humble beginnings in a small cottage, was a testament to this steadfastness. Her will wasn't deterred by the poverty of her surroundings, nor the scorn from segments of the community. Instead, it was fortified, rooted in the knowledge that she was fighting for a cause greater than herself.

Staying true to one's path also involves the ability to adapt to circumstances without compromising the core mission. In Mary's case, the relocation of the school to Hell's Hole, the garbage dump, was a harsh reality that many would have viewed as a setback. But Dr. Bethune perceived it as an opportunity. The choice to see potential where others saw despair was a testament to her unwavering will. It is in these moments that the strength of one's resolve is truly tested when faced with an obstacle that seemingly derails one's progress, but in truth, offers a different route to the same destination.

Moreover, unwavering will involves garnering support and rallying others to join the cause. Mary understood the power of community and the role it played in fortifying her mission. She rallied parents, community members, and even the unexpected allies from the gambling houses and honky tonk owners, illustrating that a shared vision can unite the most diverse of groups. In this unity, she found the strength to persist, demonstrating the ripple effect a single unwavering will can create.

Equally important is the ability to maintain hope in the face of adversity. Mary's indomitable spirit stemmed from her deep-seated belief that God was guiding her, assuring her that her cause was righteous. This reliance on faith served as her beacon, illuminating her path during the darkest times and instilling in her the courage to continue.

Drawing parallels from the present, we can look to Oprah Winfrey's Leadership Academy as another example of unwavering will. Oprah faced significant criticism and skepticism when she embarked on her mission to establish the academy. Nevertheless, she stayed true to her path, anchored by her unwavering will to provide quality education to underprivileged girls in South Africa. Like Mary, Oprah demonstrated that it is the strength of one's will, and the unyielding belief in the cause, that ultimately manifests into reality.

So, what can we learn from these trailblazing women? That the road to accomplishing great things is often rugged, and fraught with trials and tribulations. But armed with an unwavering will, even the most formidable obstacles can be overcome. It is this steadfastness, this refusal to yield to the enormity of the challenge, that distinguishes those who merely dream from those who achieve.

As we navigate the winding path of life, may we, like Mary Bethune and Oprah Winfrey, draw strength from our mission, adapt to our circumstances, rally our communities, and remain hopeful in the face of adversity. In the next section, we'll delve into the power of transformative tenacity, persevering through the most formidable adversities.

Transformative Tenacity: Persevering Through Adversity

Mary Bethune's life was a living embodiment of the transformative power of tenacity. Not only did her enduring spirit propel her own journey, but it also galvanized a revolution, sparking a wave of transformation that still resonates today. tenacity, as we can learn from Mary's story, is a grittier and more persistent form of perseverance. It is the ability to hold fast in the face of obstacles and challenges, to remain anchored when the winds of adversity threaten to uproot our foundations. It is this relentless drive to never back down, no matter how formidable the opposition, that characterizes transformative tenacity.

When Mary found herself negotiating for a garbage dump to establish her school, she was not deterred by the circumstances. She saw beyond the surface and envisioned the transformation that could occur. The adversity of the situation only fueled her tenacity, reinforcing her resolve to establish a school for African-American children. This act exemplifies the power of transformative tenacity, illustrating how adversity can become a catalyst for change when met with unwavering determination.

Furthermore, transformative tenacity often involves finding unique and innovative solutions to overcome hurdles. Mary's creative fundraising strategies, such as selling homemade sweet potato pies and forming a children's choir, demonstrate how adversity can foster creativity and resourcefulness. When confronted with the harsh reality of needing funds, she did not falter. Instead, her tenacity drove her to find solutions, however unconventional they may have been.

Similarly, we can look to the Leadership Academy for Girls, established by Oprah Winfrey, as another example of transformative tenacity. Oprah faced significant hurdles in her journey, from navigating cultural norms and societal prejudices to confronting logistical challenges and criticism. Yet, her tenacity was unwavering. Today, the academy stands as a testament to her enduring spirit, transforming the lives of countless young women.

The story of transformative tenacity is not just about overcoming adversity, but also about the profound impact it can have on those around us. Just as Mary's tenacity transformed her school and community, so too did it inspire others to adopt the same relentless spirit. Her story became a beacon of hope, radiating the transformative power of tenacity and serving as a reminder that adversity is not an end, but a beginning of something new and potentially extraordinary.

In understanding this, we too can harness the power of transformative tenacity in our own lives. We can take inspiration from these trailblazers, recognizing that it is often our most challenging experiences that shape us, refining us into more resilient and tenacious individuals. By choosing to persevere, holding steadfast in our convictions, and pushing against the tide of adversity, we too can spark transformation within ourselves and our communities.

In the final section of this chapter, we will reflect on the lessons learned from Mary McLeod Bethune and Oprah Winfrey's unwavering courage, visionary mission, indomitable faith, and transformative tenacity. We will also consider actionable steps we can take to channel these qualities in our own lives. As we navigate our own journeys, may we always remember that with tenacity, even the most formidable challenges can become opportunities for profound transformation.

Preparing to Soar With the Eagles

In this chapter, we have witnessed the courage, vision, faith, and tenacity that marked the remarkable life of Mary McLeod Bethune. Her story serves as a beacon, illuminating the path of transformation that can arise from the depths of adversity. Just like Mary, influential women like Oprah Winfrey have also channeled their inner strength to enact positive change. These stories underscore the immense potential within each of us to not only overcome challenges but also to create lasting impact. With this in mind, we present the following action steps inspired by Mary Bethune's extraordinary life:

1.

   Define Your Mission: Just like Mary Bethune, each of us must have a clear and compelling mission that guides our actions. Take time to reflect on what you truly care about. What change do you want to make in the world or in your community? Write down your mission and keep it somewhere you can see daily.

2.

Cultivate Courage: Courage is not the absence of fear, but the ability to act in the face of it. Consider the fears or doubts holding you back. Acknowledge them, and then make a plan to act despite these fears. Like Mary, choose to step forward even when the path is uncertain.

3.

Harness Your Faith: Believe in your mission and your ability to make a difference. Like Mary did with her school, imagine the potential of your own ventures. Trust in the unseen and have faith that your efforts will bear fruit.

4.

Tenacity: When faced with obstacles, remember Mary's enduring spirit. Refuse to be deterred by adversity. Instead, let it fuel your resolve. When things get tough, choose to persevere.

5.

Become a Force for Transformation: Like Mary and Oprah, use your mission, courage, faith, and tenacity to create meaningful change. Remember, transformation often starts small, but with persistence, it can ripple outwards and bring about a profound impact.

As we journey onward, let us remember the lessons of Mary McLeod Bethune's life. May her story of courage, visionary mission, unwavering faith, and transformative tenacity inspire us to meet our own challenges head-on and to become catalysts for change in our own unique ways.

7 Affirmations for Chapter 2

1. "I am inspired by the strength and vision of Black icons, and I channel their courage into my every endeavor."
2. "Every challenge I face is an opportunity to grow, just as Dr. Bethune transformed obstacles into stepping stones."
3. "With unwavering faith, I am capable of achieving my mission, even when the path seems uncertain."
4. "I stand on the shoulders of great Black leaders, drawing from their wisdom and resilience to forge my unique path."
5. "Just as Dr. Bethune persevered through adversity, I too am fortified with transformative tenacity, turning my dreams into realities."
6. "In the legacy of Black heroes, I find the motivation to remain authentic to myself and the inspiration to discover my deeper purpose."
7. "Empowered by the achievements of those who came before me, I take confident strides towards my goals, knowing I am part of a rich tapestry of Black excellence."

Knowledge Brings About Peace but Also Strategy
Dr.Evelyn - Creator

Chapter 3

Empowering Education: Elevating Through Knowledge

The journey of Dr. Mary McLeod Bethune's life is like a riveting tapestry woven with threads of resilience, determination, and an unwavering faith in the transformative power of education. It was a crisp October morning in 1904 when Dr. Bethune, armed with $1.50 and a heart filled with ambition, founded the Daytona Literary and Industrial Training Institute for Negro Girls in Daytona Beach, Florida. This venture was not just a school but a beacon of hope that defied the rampant racial and gender inequalities of the time.

In the heart of the segregated South, Dr. Bethune was confronted with significant hurdles. The oppressive Jim Crow laws and widespread racial discrimination hindered her ability to secure resources and support for her institution. The shadow of doubt loomed large, but Dr. Bethune remained unfazed. Instead, she drew strength from adversity, using it as a catalyst to turn her audacious dream into reality. Her problem was clear – the creation and growth of an institution dedicated to the education of Black girls in an environment hostile to such aspirations.

But she was not to be deterred. Using her wit, resourcefulness, and tenacity, she utilized unconventional methods to solve her problem. Rummaging through junk heaps, bargaining with merchants, and leveraging the generosity of local businesses, Dr. Bethune gathered necessary materials to keep her school operational. It was this unshakeable spirit that carried her forward, propelling the growth of the institute, and in time, it caught the attention of James M. Gamble of the Procter and Gamble Company, who became a significant benefactor.

The spark she ignited in Daytona Beach continued to burn bright and fierce. Her relentless pursuit culminated in a significant event in 1923 when her school merged with the all-male Cookman Institute of Jacksonville, Florida. This merger led to the birth of the Bethune-Cookman College, a higher education institution that stood as a testament to Dr. Bethune's conviction and dedication.

Now, imagine that, a Black woman, born to parents who had been slaves, standing at the helm of a college in the early 20th century America! Her story is one of triumph over adversity, a testament to the indomitable spirit of a woman who dared to dream beyond the limitations of her circumstances.

When we look at the modern world, we see echoes of Dr. Bethune's spirit in the story of Malala Yousafzai, a young Pakistani girl who, despite living in a region fraught with terrorism and gender inequality, fought valiantly for girls' right to education. Shot by the Taliban for her beliefs, she emerged stronger, ultimately becoming the youngest-ever Nobel Prize laureate.

Both Dr. Bethune's and Malala's stories remind us of the transformative power of education. They were not just seeking personal growth; they were setting precedents and laying the groundwork for the generations that followed.

In this chapter, we will delve deeper into Dr. Bethune's life and her unwavering belief in education. We will explore the four pillars that were integral to her mission:

1. Pursuing Progress: The Power of Lifelong Learning.
2. Wisdom and Wealth: Investing in Personal Growth.
3. Mentorship Matters: Finding and Providing Guidance.
4. Knowledge as a Catalyst: Spreading Inspiration.

The promise this chapter holds for you, dear reader, is the realization that, like Dr. Bethune and Malala, you too have the power to transform not only your life but also the lives of those around you through education and lifelong learning. Let's step forward together on this enlightening journey.

Pursuing Progress: The Power of Lifelong Learning

Dr. Mary McLeod Bethune was no stranger to the potent power of lifelong learning. She understood that education wasn't merely a tool for advancement; it was a stepping stone towards individual freedom, empowerment, and societal transformation. Driven by this understanding, she dedicated her life to breaking down educational barriers for African Americans. And, through this unwavering commitment, she built a legacy that continues to inspire today.

Born the fifteenth of seventeen children, Dr. Bethune had a distinct advantage compared to many African Americans following the Civil War - she had the chance to attend school. While this opportunity was a rarity at the time, Dr. Bethune recognized its value and seized it with an eagerness that would lay the foundation for her life's journey. This early interaction with learning wasn't just an event but a spark that lit a passion for knowledge, one that would drive her to become a beacon of hope and empowerment for her community.

As a young girl, Dr. Bethune would walk miles to attend school, determined not to let distance deter her quest for knowledge. She showed that pursuing progress through learning was not a mere act but a potent form of resistance against oppressive systems of her time. This unyielding commitment to education helped her see beyond her circumstances, pushing her to dream big and strive for more. As she grew, she realized that she was not just learning for herself, but for her community and future generations.

As she honed her skills as a teacher in Georgia and South Carolina, Dr. Bethune was consistently led by the principle of lifelong learning. Teaching was not just a job for her, but a mission - a mission to inspire others to recognize the transformative power of education, to motivate them to persist in the face of adversity, and to cultivate in them the will to strive for their dreams.

And so, in 1904, when she founded the Daytona Literary and Industrial Training Institute for Negro Girls, she did more than just provide education; she facilitated a space for growth and self-discovery. The school was not merely a place of rote learning, but a sanctuary where Black girls could imagine and aspire for a future that seemed unattainable in the world outside. It became a place where the seeds of dreams were sown and nurtured.

In creating an institution focused on education, Dr. Bethune didn't just construct a building; she built a community. She promoted a culture of learning where knowledge wasn't simply bestowed but shared and cultivated. She championed a space where each individual was not just a student, but a contributor to the learning process. This unique approach transformed the institute from an educational organization into a vital center for community growth and development.

Yet, Dr. Bethune's vision went beyond the walls of her institute. She envisioned a world where education was not the privilege of a few but the birthright of all. She saw the role of education in eradicating social and economic disparities and understood that learning was the most potent weapon to challenge the status quo.

In this journey of lifelong learning, Dr. Bethune wasn't just a pioneer; she was a pathfinder, forging a trail for others to follow. She was an advocate, tirelessly campaigning for the rights of African Americans to quality education. But most importantly, she was a testament to the transformative power of lifelong learning. Her life and her actions showed the world that education wasn't just about the accumulation of knowledge but about using that knowledge to uplift oneself and others.

The spirit of Dr. Bethune's quest for lifelong learning continues to inspire and challenge us today. It beckons us to recognize education as a vehicle of personal and societal transformation, to see learning as a journey rather than a destination, and to understand that our commitment to this journey has the power to change not just our lives but the world.

As we consider Dr. Bethune's commitment to lifelong learning, it's imperative that we apply this principle in our own lives. Like her, we can commit to continually growing, evolving, and acquiring new knowledge, regardless of our age or status. The importance of this principle lies in the understanding that the quest for knowledge does not end with a degree or diploma; it is a continuous pursuit that propels us toward personal and professional growth.

In our rapidly changing world, the ability to adapt and evolve is more crucial than ever. As technology advances, the job market evolves, and societal norms shift, it is the individuals who commit to lifelong learning who will remain relevant and adaptable. By continually expanding our knowledge and skills, we not only enrich our personal and professional lives but also equip ourselves to contribute meaningfully to our communities and societies.

However, pursuing lifelong learning isn't just about personal advantage. It's about becoming active contributors to the world around us. With every new skill we acquire, every piece of knowledge we glean, and every perspective we consider, we broaden our understanding of the world. We become more empathetic, more understanding, and more capable of making a positive impact.

Like Dr. Bethune, we can use our knowledge to dismantle barriers, challenge stereotypes, and enact change. By seeking knowledge and understanding, we position ourselves to disrupt oppressive systems, advocate for social justice, and champion equality.

In many ways, our pursuit of lifelong learning is an act of empowerment. As we learn, we grow. And as we grow, we develop the ability to shape our destinies and impact our world.

Drawing inspiration from Dr. Bethune's story, Malala Yousafzai, a young Pakistani activist, has also demonstrated the transformative power of education. Despite the oppressive Taliban regime that barred girls from education, Malala insisted on learning. She not only pursued her education but also became a staunch advocate for girls' education worldwide. Her relentless fight for educational rights echoes Dr. Bethune's belief in the transformative power of learning. Both women, though from different eras and continents, convey the same message: education is a potent tool for transformation, growth, and empowerment.

As we continue on this journey, let us keep in mind that our education, much like Dr. Bethune's and Malala's, isn't merely a pathway to personal success. It's a torch we carry, casting light on societal issues, inspiring others, and leaving a lasting impact. In the next sections, we'll delve deeper into the profound impact of investing in personal growth, the significance of mentorship, and the transformative power of spreading inspiration through knowledge.

Wisdom and Wealth: Investing in Personal Growth

Dr. Mary McLeod Bethune was not just a woman, but a beacon of light whose shine has illuminated the paths of generations, long past her time. Her life is a testament to the transformative power of education and an enduring conviction in personal growth. Born as one among seventeen children to former slaves, she was no stranger to hardship. But even the harsh walls of adversity could not contain her spirit, her desire to learn, her hunger for knowledge.

Much like a seed that begins its journey beneath the darkened soil, only to sprout, grow, and eventually tower into a colossal tree, Bethune's journey, too, was one of transformation. Her humble beginnings did not define her future, but rather, it was her will, her indomitable spirit, and her lifelong commitment to personal growth and learning that shaped her destiny. She understood the power of investing in oneself, and she harnessed it to transform not only her life but also the lives of those around her.

Today, as we stand at the crossroads of an ever-evolving world, the significance of personal growth is more pronounced than ever before. In an age of infinite knowledge at our fingertips, the opportunity for self-improvement and growth is vast and varied. Yet, the abundance of knowledge also presents a challenge. It calls for discernment, for the discipline to sift through the noise, and hone in on meaningful learning. It calls for a genuine commitment to self-improvement and personal development.

Investing in personal growth is a conscious decision to cultivate our minds and hearts, to not merely exist, but to strive continuously towards becoming the best versions of ourselves. It is about nurturing our curiosity, challenging our limitations, and stretching the boundaries of our comfort zones. It is about a relentless pursuit of wisdom and understanding, not as a means to an end but as an end in itself.

When we invest in our personal growth, we cultivate a wealth of wisdom that transcends the materialistic confines of society. This wisdom, much like a radiant jewel, shines brightest in times of adversity, guiding us forward and illuminating our path. It equips us with the resilience to navigate the storms of life and the empathy to understand those around us. This wisdom is not a static entity but a dynamic force that grows with us, evolving and deepening with each new experience and learning.

Moreover, our personal growth does not exist in isolation. It influences those around us, creating a ripple effect that can transform communities and societies. Just as Bethune's commitment to personal growth led her to create a legacy of change and empowerment, so too can our personal development drive collective progress. It can inspire others, challenge societal norms, and contribute to a broader understanding of our world.

But how do we invest in our personal growth? How do we cultivate this wealth of wisdom? The answers lie not in grand gestures but in everyday choices. It is about dedicating time each day to learning, embracing new experiences with an open mind, listening to diverse perspectives, and engaging in meaningful dialogue. It is about nurturing our mental, emotional, and spiritual well-being and recognizing that every aspect of our lives contributes to our growth.

As we continue this journey of self-discovery and personal growth, let us carry with us the legacy of Dr. Mary McLeod Bethune. Let us remember her indomitable spirit, her relentless pursuit of education, and her unwavering belief in the transformative power of personal growth. As we step into the next section, we will delve into the importance of mentorship, a pivotal aspect of personal growth and a cornerstone of Bethune's legacy.

Mentorship Matters: Finding and Providing Guidance

The legacy of Dr. Mary McLeod Bethune is not solely rooted in her achievements or the institutions she established. Rather, her impact is profoundly manifested in the lives of those she mentored and influenced. As a teacher, Bethune demonstrated that mentorship is an essential ingredient in the journey of personal growth and transformation.

Mentorship – the guidance offered by an experienced and trusted person – creates a bridge between knowledge and application, potential and realization. A mentor, much like a lighthouse, provides guidance and sheds light on the path forward, enabling us to navigate through the often turbulent seas of life. In Dr. Bethune's case, her role as a mentor extended beyond imparting academic knowledge; she shared life skills, instilled values, and cultivated leadership. She acted as an exemplary mentor by leveraging her wisdom and experience to create a roadmap for success for her students.

To appreciate the profound impact of mentorship, let's delve into why mentorship matters in our quest for personal growth and transformation. A mentor aids in illuminating our strengths, shedding light on areas for improvement, and navigating career paths or life choices. They provide the benefit of their experiences and wisdom, saving us from potential pitfalls and guiding us to make more informed decisions. Furthermore, mentors challenge us, pushing us beyond our comfort zones and enabling us to reach new heights of personal and professional development.

Like Dr. Bethune, mentors also offer emotional support and encouragement, fostering resilience and self-belief in the face of adversity. They serve as living proof of what is possible, instilling hope and driving us to strive for excellence.

As important as finding mentorship is offering it. Just as a tree disperses seeds far and wide, mentors have the opportunity to influence countless lives beyond their immediate sphere. Dr. Bethune, through her mentorship, impacted not only the lives of her direct students but also the countless lives they subsequently touched. This ripple effect of mentorship underscores its transformative power and the imperative for each of us to pass on the wisdom and guidance we receive.

Dr. Bethune's life serves as a clarion call for each of us to be both recipients and providers of mentorship. Whether it is a teacher, a supervisor, a family member, or a peer, we all have the capacity to find and offer guidance. Furthermore, mentorship isn't a one-size-fits-all approach; it is as diverse and unique as the individuals involved. Each mentor-mentee relationship is a unique confluence of experiences, perspectives, and lessons that collectively aid in personal and communal growth.

As we explore our paths of personal growth, let us recognize and embrace the value of mentorship. Let us seek out those who can guide us, and in turn, share our knowledge and experiences with others. As we carry forward the legacy of Dr. Mary McLeod Bethune, we remember that mentorship is more than just teaching and learning; it's about empowering, inspiring, and transforming lives.

As we move into the next section, we will examine how knowledge acts as a catalyst for inspiration, a concept intimately familiar to Dr. Bethune and central to her life's mission.

Knowledge as a Catalyst: Spreading Inspiration

In Dr. Mary McLeod Bethune's world, knowledge wasn't a mere commodity; it was a powerful catalyst that could inspire, uplift, and transform lives. Knowledge had the ability to ignite minds, fostering a spark that would burn bright, illuminating the path forward for oneself and others. In this section, we delve into how knowledge acts as a catalyst and explore the importance of spreading inspiration.

Dr. Bethune was a staunch believer in the transformative power of education. She understood that knowledge wasn't static or isolated. Instead, it was dynamic and interconnected, constantly evolving, and perpetually expanding. She knew that every piece of knowledge had the potential to be a stepping stone towards greater understanding, a deeper connection with the world, and an enhanced ability to contribute to society.

In the hands of Dr. Bethune, knowledge became a tool to inspire and empower. She used her knowledge to confront systemic racism and advocate for equal educational opportunities. She leveraged it to establish educational institutions that would stand as bastions of hope and progress. And she wielded it to inspire her students, fellow citizens, and the entire nation towards the pursuit of justice and equality.

Inspiration is a powerful force. It ignites our passion, fuels our creativity, and propels us towards our goals. When we're inspired, we're not just dreaming; we're driven to act, to contribute, and to make a difference. In essence, inspiration is the bridge between knowledge and action. When knowledge inspires us, it triggers a domino effect of positive change that extends far beyond ourselves.

As carriers of knowledge, we have a responsibility to spread inspiration. Every nugget of wisdom, every lesson learned, and every piece of insight gained has the potential to inspire someone else. Just as Dr. Bethune did, we can use our knowledge to inspire others, encouraging them to pursue their passions, overcome their challenges, and strive for their dreams.

Spreading inspiration isn't limited to grand gestures or large-scale initiatives. It can be as simple as sharing an enlightening book, speaking words of encouragement, or exemplifying resilience in the face of adversity. Each act, no matter how small, has the potential to create ripples of inspiration that can reach far and wide.

Dr. Bethune's life was a testament to the incredible power of knowledge as a catalyst for inspiration. As we journey towards personal growth and transformation, let us remember her legacy and strive to use our knowledge to inspire others. As we learn, grow, and evolve, let's endeavor to light the way for those who follow, just as Dr. Bethune did.

In the concluding section, we will summarize the key points discussed in this chapter and provide actionable steps to integrate these lessons into our lives, in alignment with the transformative legacy of Dr. Mary McLeod Bethune.

A Blueprint for Transformation

In this chapter, we journeyed through the incredible life of Dr. Mary McLeod Bethune, tracing her path from a humble background to becoming a towering figure in the annals of American history. Her story illuminates the transformative power of education, personal growth, mentorship, and the catalytic role of knowledge in inspiring and creating change.

As we draw this chapter to a close, let's crystallize the significant lessons we've gleaned.

Firstly, we learned about the power of lifelong learning. Dr. Bethune's journey reaffirmed that the quest for knowledge is a lifelong endeavor, one that continually opens doors to growth and progress. It's a catalyst for personal transformation that expands our horizons and enriches our lives.

Secondly, we delved into the significance of investing in personal growth. Wisdom and personal development are intrinsically linked. When we invest in ourselves, we nurture the seeds of wisdom that have been planted within us, enabling us to flourish and make a difference in our lives and those of others.

Thirdly, we appreciated the essential role of mentorship. Dr. Bethune's life underscored the immense value of having and being a mentor. By providing and seeking guidance, we create a nurturing environment for personal and collective growth.

Finally, we examined how knowledge can act as a catalyst for spreading inspiration. Dr. Bethune exemplified how the acquisition and dissemination of knowledge could serve as a beacon of inspiration, encouraging others to strive for greatness.

Now that we've imbibed these lessons, it's time to put them into practice. Here are five action steps that you can start implementing today:

1. Embrace Lifelong Learning: Commit to being a lifelong learner. Make it a goal to learn something new every day, whether it's a skill, a fact, a perspective, or a piece of wisdom.
2. Invest in Personal Growth: Invest time, effort, and resources into your personal development. Attend workshops, read books, seek counseling, or join a group that aligns with your growth objectives.
3. Seek and Provide Mentorship: Find a mentor who can guide you on your journey and be willing to mentor others. Sharing knowledge and experience is a two-way street that benefits both the mentor and the mentee.
4. Spread Inspiration: Use your knowledge to inspire others. Share your insights, wisdom, and experiences to motivate others towards their goals.
5. Reflect and Act: Make time for reflection. Evaluate your progress regularly and adjust your strategies as necessary.

As we follow in the footsteps of Dr. Bethune, let's commit to embracing education, pursuing personal growth, seeking and offering mentorship, and spreading inspiration. By doing so, we can honor her legacy and foster our transformation, leading lives of purpose, achievement, and impact.

Remember, you are the architect of your destiny. With the Bethune Blueprint in hand, you have the power to design a life of greatness. Let the journey of transformation begin.

7 Affirmations for Chapter 3: Empowering Education: Elevating Through Knowledge

1. "Each day, I absorb knowledge that empowers and enlightens my journey, honoring the path paved by Dr. Bethune."
2. "In the legacy of great Black icons, I am constantly reminded that with determination and education, no dream is too vast."
3. "The wisdom of the past fuels my future. Every lesson I learn is a step towards my purpose."
4. "I am connected to a rich heritage of Black educators and trailblazers; their strength and resilience inspire my daily endeavors."
5. "Through education, I elevate not only myself but my community, ensuring the stories of our heroes continue to be told and celebrated."
6. "Knowledge is my compass, guiding me towards self-discovery, purpose, and empowerment."
7. "Like Dr. Mary McLeod Bethune, I am a beacon of hope, transformation, and continuous growth, dedicated to leaving a lasting legacy."

REMEMBER WHEN WE COULD FLY
DrEvelyn - Creator

Chapter 4

Resilient Resonance: Rising Above Strife

In the grand tapestry of history, certain figures rise like beacons, their stories guiding lights for generations to come. Dr. Mary McLeod Bethune is undeniably one such beacon. Her spirit was forged in resilience, her legacy a testament to the power of determination, and her life a lesson in transformative change. We will delve into her inspiring narrative in this chapter, drawing comparisons to the adversities faced by contemporary women and gleaning wisdom from her struggles and triumphs.

Born as the fifteenth child to former slaves in South Carolina in 1875, merely a decade after the American Civil War, Dr. Bethune was no stranger to adversity. Racial discrimination was rife, and opportunities were scarce for Black Americans. Yet, a spark ignited within her heart, an unyielding aspiration for a world where education wasn't a privilege but a right for every Black child, especially girls.

Our journey starts at a critical juncture in her life, an instance that tested her resolve like no other. She had managed to start a school for Black girls, but its growth necessitated more land, a hurdle that proved almost insurmountable in the early 1900s. In this era, women, regardless of their race, were expected to confine themselves within domesticity, their voices often silenced and their dreams overlooked. Women didn't have the right to vote; their destinies were tightly tethered to men's will.

For Black women, the struggle was intensified, trapped at the intersection of race and gender discrimination. Dr. Bethune, despite these societal constraints, embarked on her quest to secure land. The only available piece she could procure was a disregarded garbage dump within the Black community. The price was set at $250, a seemingly unattainable sum for a Black woman with limited resources in that period.

Yet, Dr. Bethune, bolstered by her unflinching faith and perseverance, persuaded the landowner, a white man, to accept payment installments. She stood at the precipice of uncertainty, yet her faith didn't waver. This leap of faith was the cornerstone upon which the Daytona Normal School for Girls was built.

Her battle was far from over. When the Ku Klux Klan, notorious for their white supremacist beliefs, decided to intimidate the school into closure, Dr. Bethune's resilience shone brighter than ever. She called upon her students, lit every light on the small campus, and filled the air with the harmonious melodies of their songs. Their music served as a fortification against the destructive intentions of the Klan. That night, not a single flame was lit, and the Klan receded, never to return.

Dr. Bethune's victory echoes in the hallways of history, reverberating into the present day, its resonance felt in movements like Black Lives Matter. Founded in 2013 by Alicia Garza, Patrisse Cullors, and Opal Tometi, the Black Lives Matter movement, much like Dr. Bethune's endeavors, champions the rights of Black individuals and raises a rallying cry against systemic racism and violence.

As we journey through this chapter, we'll delve into four pivotal facets that encapsulated
Dr. Bethune's struggle. We will explore the following four points:

1. Braving Barriers: Confronting Injustice
2. Steadfast Spirit: Cultivating Inner Fortitude
3. Empathetic Engagement: Connecting with Others
4. Unified Uprising: Mobilizing for Change

Each of these sections will present a profound lesson, a stepping stone on your path to transformation. Let us step forward in this journey, taking with us Dr. Bethune's resilience, courage, and unwavering belief in the power of change.

Braving Barriers: Confronting Injustice

In her heart, Mary McLeod Bethune knew she had a mission. Not one of self-service or ease, but a call to arms in the face of towering societal injustices. When she looked at her world, she didn't see insurmountable walls of racial prejudice and gender discrimination; instead, she saw barriers to be overcome, and challenges to be braved. This section of our journey delves into Dr. Bethune's confrontation with these barriers.

In the early 1900s, as a Black woman in a deeply segregated and discriminatory society, Mary was expected to succumb to societal norms that allowed her limited rights and freedoms. She lived in a world where her voice was muted, her dreams ridiculed, and her worth defined by her race and gender. But, the mission ignited within her refused to be quelled.

Dr. Bethune faced countless racial and gender barriers. She lived during a time when racial segregation was codified into law, where Jim Crow laws stifled the rights and opportunities of Black people, and where gender norms limited the roles of women, especially Black women, to strictly domestic duties. But, Mary was not one to bow down to societal pressure. Instead, she believed that education was the key to unlocking the shackles of oppression.

Let's consider the incident of the land purchase for her school. Mary was offered the least desirable piece of land, a garbage dump, simply because of the color of her skin. The discrimination she faced was explicit, the racism unapologetic. But did she allow this to dissuade her? No. She saw potential where others saw despair. She perceived this challenge as an opportunity, and with steadfast determination, she turned a garbage dump into a thriving institution for Black girls. Her unwavering commitment demonstrated how she continually braved barriers of injustice.

Mary understood the profound importance of education, not just as a means of personal growth but also as a tool for societal transformation. Her faith in her mission and her relentless spirit fueled her courage to confront these systemic barriers head-on. The garbage dump was not a deterring barrier but a stepping stone toward her goal.

Just like Dr. Bethune, we face our own barriers. They may not come in the form of explicit racial or gender discrimination. They might be subtle, concealed in the fabric of our everyday lives. Perhaps they're in the form of societal expectations or personal doubts and fears. It's critical for us to recognize these barriers and develop the courage to brave them.

Black Lives Matter, a movement born out of the modern-day struggle against racial injustice, parallels Mary's resilience. When we look at the Black Lives Matter movement, we witness a collective confrontation against racial injustice. Its founders, Alicia Garza, Patrisse Cullors, and Opal Tometi, refused to remain silent in the face of persistent racial discrimination and violence. The movement, similar to Dr. Bethune's stand against injustice, is an uprising against racial barriers, a demand for equality, respect, and dignity.

There is a shared spirit of bravery between Dr. Mary McLeod Bethune and the founders of the Black Lives Matter movement. Their stories serve as potent reminders of our capacity to face and overcome societal barriers, urging us to confront injustices in our own lives and communities.

Dr. Bethune's life offers a blueprint to face our own challenges. We can carry forward her legacy by recognizing the barriers in our lives and braving them with the same spirit of resilience. As we journey through this chapter, we will explore how to cultivate this steadfast spirit, engage empathetically with others, and mobilize for change, just like Mary did.

Steadfast Spirit: Cultivating Inner Fortitude

While external forces often pose formidable challenges, Mary McLeod Bethune's story shows us that it's our inner strength that ultimately determines our resilience. The courage to face adversity is born from a steadfast spirit, an inner fortitude that empowers us to rise above the trials we encounter.

Dr. Bethune's inner fortitude was remarkable. Her strong faith and relentless determination served as the foundation for her fight against racial and gender discrimination. She held an unwavering belief in her mission and a dogged refusal to let external circumstances dictate her actions.

Consider the event of the impending attack by the KKK on her school. The mere rumor of such an attack would have sent many into a spiral of fear. However, Dr. Bethune's response was nothing short of extraordinary. Instead of letting fear consume her and her students, she instructed her pupils to sing. In the face of threats, she stood firm, drawing on her inner strength. She transformed what could have been a moment of despair into an act of courage, a testament to her incredible inner fortitude.

This is the type of strength that we need in our own lives. Life, as we know, is not devoid of challenges. We face adversity in many forms – it could be personal struggles, professional setbacks, societal injustices, or even battles within ourselves. In the face of these trials, it is our inner strength that sees us through. Cultivating this steadfast spirit is not an overnight process. It requires a deep understanding of ourselves and our values, a strong sense of purpose, and a determined resolve to persevere despite the odds.

The spirit of resilience displayed by Dr. Bethune resonates with the strength demonstrated by the founders of the Black Lives Matter movement. In response to the pervasive issue of racial violence, they fostered a movement that shook the world. This movement did not stem from a place of external power but from an inner strength, a steadfast spirit that refused to be silenced in the face of injustice.

Alicia Garza, Patrisse Cullors, and Opal Tometi – the women behind Black Lives Matter – each faced their own personal trials and societal barriers. Yet, they remained undeterred, rallying millions across the globe to join their cause. Like Mary, they demonstrated the power of a steadfast spirit in bringing about change.

Empathetic Engagement: Connecting with Others

We have explored the power of resolute spirit and steadfastness in the face of adversity. Yet, our journey toward personal greatness isn't confined to our individual spirit; it involves our relationships with others, how we connect, and how we empathize. It's about embracing the humanity that binds us all in a shared experience. Dr. Mary McLeod Bethune exemplified this in her unwavering dedication to her students and her community.

Imagine the scene on that fateful night when the KKK threatened to raze her school. The fear would have been palpable. The uncertainty of the night gnawing at the hearts of each child. Yet, in this moment, Mary McLeod Bethune, daughter of Samuel and Patsy McLeod, did not distance herself from the terror; instead, she drew closer to her students, using the power of empathetic engagement to stoke an act of collective courage in the face of impending danger.

She assembled them all, not hiding away in the safety of her room, nor sending her students away to face the fear alone. Mary stood with them, fully present in their shared fear, their shared uncertainty, and their shared determination. This shared emotional space created an atmosphere of empathy, solidarity, and collective resilience, a force so strong that it withstood the impending threat.

This experience wasn't about eliminating fear; it was about facing it together, transforming it into a catalyst for unity and strength. Empathetic engagement involves stepping into someone else's shoes, understanding their feelings, and connecting with them on a human level. This engagement is transformative; it engenders trust, nurtures unity, and ultimately, leads to collective empowerment.

In our personal journey toward greatness, cultivating empathy is crucial. Empathy enables us to form deep, meaningful connections with others, understand their perspectives, and validate their experiences. It fosters a sense of belonging and creates a safe space for open, authentic communication. It strengthens our relationships, opening the door for collaboration, mutual support, and shared success.

Just as Mary used empathetic engagement to stand with her students, we can use it to stand with those around us. We can create a nurturing environment that supports growth, resilience, and collective strength. We can build bridges of understanding, challenging the divides of race, class, gender, and other socio-cultural constructs that often alienate us from one another.

Through empathetic engagement, we honor the human dignity in others, aligning ourselves with the core values of respect, understanding, and equality. And in doing so, we align ourselves with the legacy of Dr. Bethune, a legacy that champions unity, empathy, and collective resilience.

As we continue our journey, let's remember that empathy is not a passive attribute; it's an active endeavor, one that requires openness, understanding, and a willingness to connect. In the next section, we will delve deeper into the transformative power of unified uprising and how we can mobilize for change in our personal lives and in our society. Shall we proceed?

As we journey through this chapter, we will draw strength from the courage exhibited by Mary and the founders of the Black Lives Matter movement. Their stories guide us in cultivating our own inner fortitude, a quality that empowers us to stand firm against the trials we encounter.

In our next section, we'll explore how our inner strength enables us to engage empathetically with others, even in the face of adversity. As Mary's story demonstrates, this ability to connect with others despite the trials we face is a testament to the strength of our spirit. It allows us to extend beyond ourselves, to reach out and inspire change in the lives of others. It's through this empathetic engagement that we truly begin to resonate with the resilient spirit of Mary McLeod Bethune.

Unified Uprising: Mobilizing for Change

Dr. Mary McLeod Bethune, through her empathetic engagement and steadfast spirit, built an unbreakable community, grounded in shared experiences, collective courage, and a profound respect for humanity. But Mary's journey was not just about building a resilient community; it was also about mobilizing this community to rise against the prevailing injustices, to spark a unified uprising that championed change. Her life's work was a testament to the transformative power of collective action.

The night the KKK threatened to burn down Mary's school, she mobilized her students and staff in a bold display of collective defiance. Their unity sent a clear message: they were unshakeable, unbreakable, and untamed by fear. The lights shone bright, and their voices echoed into the night, creating a powerful harmony that drowned the venomous threats of the oppressors.

It was a testament to Mary's leadership and her belief in the power of unity. By standing together, they had effectively turned the tide against their oppressors. Mary understood the necessity of collective action in the face of systemic injustice, and she leveraged this understanding to mobilize her community toward positive change.

Mary's legacy teaches us that achieving personal greatness is not an isolated journey. It's an interdependent process that involves standing up for each other, standing up for justice, and standing up for change. It requires us to mobilize ourselves and those around us, fostering a collective spirit of resilience, empathy, and action.

In our pursuit of personal transformation, we must ask ourselves: How can we spark a unified uprising in our own lives? How can we mobilize for change?

The answer lies in leveraging our individual strengths and the strength of our community. By recognizing the barriers we face and the systemic injustices that persist, we can begin to challenge these structures, advocating for change, and taking active steps towards building a more equitable society.

In doing so, we align ourselves with the legacy of Dr. Bethune. We embody her spirit of unity, resilience, and change. We carry forward her dream of a society grounded in equality, respect, and mutual empowerment.

As we conclude this chapter, we find ourselves at a crossroads. We can choose to follow Mary's path, bravely confronting our barriers, cultivating inner fortitude, connecting empathetically with others, and mobilizing for change, or we can choose to remain passive, letting the waves of life steer our course.

Strength Born from Struggle

In this chapter, we've embarked on a remarkable journey, tracing the footsteps of Dr. Mary McLeod Bethune. We've traversed the pathways she courageously paved, navigating through a racially divided landscape, and have come face to face with the relentless spirit that propelled her to rise above the societal strife of her time.

Despite the perilous threats from the KKK and opposition from the white community, Dr. Bethune stood her ground, exhibiting an awe-inspiring blend of bravery and tenacity. Her actions weren't just about the survival of the Daytona Normal School for Girls; they were about setting an example, a precedent, a testament to the unconquerable spirit of Black women. She established an indelible standard of resilience that echoes through the annals of Black history, whispering strength into the hearts of Black women today.

As we reflect on Dr. Bethune's story, we are reminded of contemporary figures like Tarana Burke, whose relentless fight against sexual violence gave rise to the Me Too Movement, a powerful beacon for survivors worldwide. These women, separated by generations, share an unyielding resilience, a resonating force that refuses to bow down to societal barriers.

In examining Dr. Bethune's life, we've unearthed key lessons about confronting injustices, cultivating inner fortitude, connecting empathetically with others, and mobilizing for change. As we digest these lessons, we are tasked to weave them into our own lives, to amplify our voices, and to continue the legacy these influential Black women have gifted us.

So, how do we apply these lessons? It begins with an acknowledgment of our individual struggles and the societal barriers before us. By recognizing these obstacles, we can strategize ways to surmount them, just as Dr. Bethune did. She teaches us that bravery isn't an absence of fear but an action taken in spite of it.

Next, we must nurture our inner spirit. The cultivation of an indomitable spirit requires constant self-affirmation and the belief in our abilities, the same belief Dr. Bethune had in herself and her mission. Remember her words, "Invest in the human soul. Who knows, it might be a diamond in the rough."

Subsequently, we have to reach out and engage with those around us empathetically. Let us lean on each other's experiences and knowledge, and foster a community that uplifts and supports, just as Dr. Bethune built her institution on the principles of sisterhood and mutual upliftment.

Lastly, we need to mobilize for change in whatever capacity we can. We might not all start movements like Tarana Burke, but each of us can contribute to the ongoing fight against racial discrimination and social inequalities. It could be as simple as advocating for diversity in our workplaces, participating in community organizations, or voicing our concerns and offering solutions to local representatives.

In conclusion, the essence of this chapter, the heart of Dr. Mary McLeod Bethune's story, lies in the testament of resilience. It's about the resounding echo of Black women's strength and unity that continues to resonate through centuries, etching a legacy of courage, resilience, and unity. This legacy is not just a symbol of our past but a beacon illuminating our path forward.

As Black women, we are not just carriers of this legacy but active contributors to its shaping. The strength of Dr. Bethune and countless other Black women exists within us. As we forge ahead on our transformative journeys, let us carry their stories in our hearts, their resilience in our spirits, and their lessons in our actions. Like Dr. Bethune, let us rise above strife and resonate resilience.

7 Affirmations for Chapter 4

1. "Like Dr. Bethune, I carry the strength of my ancestors within me, empowering me to rise above any challenge that comes my way."
2. "Every obstacle I encounter is an opportunity for growth, transformation, and deepening resilience."
3. "Just as Dr. Bethune transformed adversity into progress, I too have the power to turn my struggles into stepping stones toward greatness."
4. "In unity with others, I find strength, wisdom, and the courage to effect change in my community and the world."
5. "I am a beacon of hope, perseverance, and determination, and my journey honors the legacy of trailblazing Black women who came before me."
6. "With unwavering faith in my purpose, I stand tall against the winds of doubt, prejudice, and fear."
7. "My narrative, like Dr. Bethune's, is one of triumph over trials, and each day I am writing a chapter of success, resilience, and lasting impact."

I AM STRONG I AM WORTHY I AM BEAUTIFUL I AM
WOMAN
DrEvelyn - Creator

Chapter 5

Sisterhood and Solidarity: Building Supportive Networks

Dr. Mary McLeod Bethune, a visionary educator, and civil rights activist, faced a daunting problem in the early 20th century. Despite her success in creating educational opportunities for African-American women, she recognized that the voices of these women were fragmented and often drowned out by the noise of a racially divided society. With unwavering faith in God and the power of sisterhood, she embarked on a mission to unite these strong, intelligent Black women under a common cause.

To solve this problem, Dr. Bethune founded the National Council of Negro Women (NCNW) in 1935. This organization provided a unified platform for African-American women to address pressing issues such as education, employment, health, and civil rights. Through the NCNW, Black women from diverse backgrounds came together to form a collective national voice that could no longer be ignored.

Dr. Bethune's determination and tireless efforts led to the establishment of the NCNW headquarters in Washington, D.C. in 1944, which became a symbol of progress and unity for African-American women across the country. The organization rapidly gained respect and influence, allowing its members to participate in crucial discussions on national events and develop programs to combat discrimination in various sectors of society.

Fast forward to today, and we see the legacy of Dr. Bethune's work embodied in influential women like Ava DuVernay, a celebrated filmmaker, and founder of ARRAY Collective. Through ARRAY, DuVernay amplifies the voices of underrepresented artists and storytellers, providing a platform for diverse narratives to be shared with the world. Just as Dr. Bethune sought to unite the voices of Black women, DuVernay brings together a community of creatives to create lasting change in the entertainment industry.

In this chapter, we will explore the four key aspects of sisterhood and solidarity that are vital to building supportive networks:

1. Bonding Bridges: Forming Lasting Connections
2. Collective Care: Nurturing Relationships
3. Empathetic Empowerment: Lifting Each Other Up
4. Strength in Sisterhood: The Power of Unity

By understanding and embracing these principles, you can create a strong, supportive network that empowers you and those around you to thrive.

Bonding Bridges: Forming Lasting Connections

The first step in building a strong sisterhood is to establish connections that bridge gaps between individuals with shared goals and experiences. Dr. Mary McLeod Bethune's vision for the National Council of Negro Women was rooted in the understanding that unity among Black women was essential for progress. By forming these bonds, the NCNW was able to foster lasting connections that still exist today.

Seek Out Shared Experiences and Common Goals

To form lasting connections, it is crucial to seek out and engage with those who share similar experiences and objectives. In Dr. Bethune's case, she gathered African-American women from diverse backgrounds and professions, united by their determination to improve the lives of Black women across America. By connecting with others who share your passions and struggles, you can create a supportive network that fuels collective growth.

Embrace Diversity and Inclusivity

One of the strengths of the NCNW was its commitment to inclusivity. Dr. Bethune recognized that a diverse group of women, representing various backgrounds and perspectives, would be more effective in addressing the multitude of issues faced by African-American women. Embracing diversity within your network not only enriches the collective experience but also fosters an environment that nurtures empathy and understanding.

Cultivate Trust and Open Communication

A key aspect of building strong connections is cultivating trust through open and honest communication. Dr. Bethune encouraged the members of the NCNW to speak their minds and engage in constructive dialogue to address the challenges they faced. By fostering a sense of trust and openness, you can create a space where individuals feel comfortable sharing their thoughts, ideas, and concerns.

Engage in Collaborative Efforts

Working together on projects and initiatives can help strengthen the connections within your network. The NCNW successfully campaigned for civil rights, education, and economic opportunities by collaborating on various programs and events. By engaging in cooperative efforts, you can not only create opportunities for individual growth but also contribute to the collective success of your network.By incorporating these elements into your approach to building connections, you can lay the foundation for a strong, supportive sisterhood that mirrors the legacy of Dr. Mary McLeod Bethune and the National Council of Negro Women.

Empowerment Through Education and Economic Opportunities

A crucial aspect of Dr. Bethune's vision for the NCNW was the empowerment of Black women through education and economic opportunities. She understood that access to education and financial independence would significantly impact the lives of African-American women and their communities. By following her example, you can work towards empowering yourself and others in your network.

Prioritize Education

Education played a pivotal role in Dr. Bethune's life, and she believed it to be the key to unlock the potential of African-American women. To empower yourself and others, prioritize education as a lifelong pursuit. Seek out opportunities for personal and professional development through formal schooling, workshops, seminars, and online courses. Encourage your network members to do the same and share resources that can help each other grow.

Support Entrepreneurship and Financial Literacy

Economic independence is essential to empowerment, and one way to achieve this is through entrepreneurship. Dr. Bethune championed this idea by encouraging Black women to start their own businesses and become financially independent. Supporting entrepreneurship within your network can help create job opportunities and contribute to community growth. Furthermore, promoting financial literacy can empower individuals to make informed decisions about their finances, leading to greater financial stability.

Advocate for Equal Opportunities and Access

Dr. Bethune fought tirelessly for equal opportunities for African-American women, understanding that systemic barriers hindered their progress. To continue her legacy, advocate for policies and initiatives that provide equal access to education, employment, and other opportunities. By using your voice and influence, you can help dismantle systemic barriers and create an environment that fosters growth and success for everyone.

Nurture Talents and Skills

Every individual possesses unique talents and skills that can contribute to the empowerment of themselves and others. Identify and nurture these talents within your network, encouraging members to use their abilities to benefit their communities. By doing so, you not only create opportunities for personal growth but also strengthen the collective impact of your network.

Celebrate Success and Foster Resilience

Empowerment also involves recognizing and celebrating successes, both big and small. Acknowledge the achievements of your network members and use their stories to inspire and motivate others. At the same time, foster resilience by sharing lessons learned from challenges and setbacks. This will create a supportive environment that encourages individuals to persevere and pursue their goals.

By prioritizing education, supporting entrepreneurship, advocating for equal opportunities, nurturing talents, and celebrating successes, you can empower yourself and others in your network, following in the footsteps of Dr. Mary McLeod Bethune and the NCNW.

Building a Supportive Network and Collaborative Partnerships

Dr. Mary McLeod Bethune understood the power of unity and collaboration in achieving the goals of the NCNW. Building a supportive network and forging collaborative partnerships can create lasting change and multiply the impact of your efforts. In this section, we'll discuss how to establish a strong network and foster meaningful collaborations.

Connect with Like-minded Individuals

The first step in building a supportive network is to connect with people who share your vision and values. Seek out individuals who are passionate about empowering African-American women and making a difference in their communities. Attend events, join online forums, and engage in conversations to identify potential members for your network.

Encourage Open Communication and Mutual Support

To create a supportive environment, encourage open communication and mutual support among network members. Foster an atmosphere where individuals feel comfortable discussing their ideas, challenges, and achievements. This will enable members to learn from each other, offer encouragement, and celebrate successes together.

Establish Clear Goals and Objectives

Having clear goals and objectives will provide direction and focus for your network. Identify specific areas where you want to make an impact, such as education, economic empowerment, or leadership development. Develop action plans to achieve these goals and regularly review your progress.

Collaborate with Other Organizations

Collaborating with other organizations can amplify the impact of your efforts and lead to more significant change. Look for opportunities to partner with groups that share your vision and have complementary resources or expertise. Together, you can achieve more than you could individually.

Develop Leadership Skills Within the Network

Empowerment begins with strong leadership. Invest in developing the leadership skills of your network members, providing them with opportunities to take on responsibility and contribute to decision-making. By doing so, you will build a strong foundation for sustainable growth and continued success.

Recognize and Address Challenges

Building a supportive network and forging collaborative partnerships come with challenges, such as differing opinions, limited resources, and competing priorities. Recognize these challenges and address them head-on, finding solutions that promote the best interests of the network and its goals.

By connecting with like-minded individuals, encouraging open communication, establishing clear goals, collaborating with other organizations, developing leadership skills, and addressing challenges, you can build a supportive network that fosters empowerment and lasting change. In doing so, you will continue the legacy of Dr. Mary McLeod Bethune and the NCNW, making a lasting impact on the lives of African-American women and their communities.

Creating a Lasting Impact through Mentorship and Community Involvement

One of Dr. Mary McLeod Bethune's most significant contributions was her dedication to mentorship and community involvement. By empowering and guiding others, she created a lasting impact on countless lives. In this section, we'll discuss the importance of mentorship and community involvement in achieving your goals and continuing the legacy of the NCNW.

The Power of Mentorship

Mentorship is a powerful tool for personal and professional growth. By sharing knowledge, experience, and guidance, mentors can help mentees navigate challenges and make informed decisions. In turn, mentees gain invaluable insights, build confidence, and develop essential skills. To create a successful mentoring relationship, seek out individuals who share your values and have the experience and skills you wish to develop. Establish clear expectations and goals for the relationship, and maintain open communication. As a mentor, be open to learning from your mentee as well, fostering a mutually beneficial partnership.

Community involvement is essential to achieving lasting change and making a meaningful impact. By engaging with local organizations, participating in community events, and advocating for the needs of African-American women, you can raise awareness and mobilize resources to address pressing issues. There are numerous ways to get involved in your community, such as volunteering, joining local committees or boards, and attending community meetings. Identify opportunities that align with your goals and the needs of the community and commit to making a difference.

Measuring and Celebrating Success

To ensure your efforts are having the desired impact, regularly evaluate your progress and the outcomes of your initiatives. Use data-driven assessments to inform your decisions and adjust your strategies as needed. Celebrate your achievements and the progress made by your network and community, recognizing the hard work and dedication that has led to success.

By embracing the power of mentorship and actively engaging in community involvement, you can create a lasting impact on the lives of African-American women and their communities. In doing so, you will honor the legacy of Dr. Mary McLeod Bethune and the NCNW, inspiring future generations to continue the fight for equality and empowerment.

Uniting to Create a Brighter Future

As we conclude our exploration of Dr. Mary McLeod Bethune's life and the National Council of Negro Women, we've seen the transformative power of a collective vision and unwavering determination. Through her relentless efforts, Dr. Bethune created a lasting legacy that continues to inspire and empower African-American women today.

- The formation of the NCNW and its impact on the lives of African-American women
- Dr. Bethune's commitment to education and advocacy for economic and social justice
- The importance of collaboration and partnerships in driving change
- The role of mentorship and community involvement in creating a lasting impact.

Taking Action

To carry forward the vision and legacy of Dr. Mary McLeod Bethune and the NCNW, consider these five action steps:

- Educate yourself: Delve deeper into the history of the NCNW and African-American women's contributions to society. Understand the challenges they faced and the solutions they implemented to create change.
- Join the NCNW or a similar organization: Connect with like-minded individuals who are committed to the empowerment of African-American women. Together, you can work towards common goals and create a more significant impact.
- Engage in mentorship: Seek out mentorship opportunities or become a mentor yourself. Sharing knowledge and experience with others is a powerful way to foster growth and development.
- Get involved in your community: Identify local organizations and initiatives that align with your passions and values. Contribute your time, skills, and resources to make a difference in your community.
- Advocate for change: Use your voice and platform to raise awareness about issues affecting African-American women. Advocate for policies and initiatives that promote equality, justice, and empowerment.

By taking these action steps, you can honor the legacy of Dr. Mary McLeod Bethune and the National Council of Negro Women, while paving the way for a brighter future for African-American women and their communities.

7 Affirmations that relate to this chapter

1. I am a powerful and influential force for change in my community, just like Dr. Mary McLeod Bethune.
2. I embrace the opportunity to learn from strong, intelligent women and to uplift others in return.

3. By connecting with like-minded individuals, I can make an even greater impact in the fight for equality and justice.

4. My faith in God and my unwavering determination propel me forward in my pursuit of empowering others.

5. I am committed to being a mentor and a mentee, nurturing growth and wisdom within myself and others.

6. As an advocate for change, I am actively using my voice and actions to create a more equitable and just world.

7. Every day, I choose to invest my time and energy in organizations and causes that align with my values and passions.

SISTAHS!
DrEvelyn

Chapter 6

Political Prowess: Advocating for Equality

In the midst of the Great Depression, a beacon of hope emerged for African Americans. Dr. Mary McLeod Bethune, a determined and dedicated Black woman, was appointed as a special advisor on minority affairs by President Franklin D. Roosevelt. As the first African-American woman to lead a federal agency, she faced the monumental challenge of advocating for the needs of her community during one of the darkest periods in American history.

Dr. Bethune had already made a name for herself as a skilled educator and civil rights activist, but this new role would test her resolve and political acumen. She was determined to prove that a Black woman could excel in a position of power and make a difference for her people.

As the Director of the National Youth Administration's (NYA) Office of Minority Affairs, Dr. Bethune faced a myriad of problems. Racial discrimination was rampant, and many young African Americans were struggling to find work during the Depression. Dr. Bethune's primary challenge was to ensure that the NYA's resources were distributed equitably so that Black youth would have a fighting chance to rise above the crushing weight of poverty.

With her signature tenacity, Dr. Bethune tackled this problem head-on. She lobbied tirelessly to expand the NYA's programs for African-American youth and fought to include anti-discrimination clauses in government contracts. Through her advocacy, she opened doors for thousands of young Black men and women, providing them with employment opportunities and a renewed sense of hope.

Her successes within the NYA paved the way for Dr. Bethune to make an even greater impact. She formed the Black Cabinet, an informal network of African-American advisors to President Roosevelt. Under her leadership, this group of dedicated professionals pressed for civil rights from within the federal government. Their efforts led to the integration of the Washington D.C. federal workforce, the expansion of New Deal relief to Black communities, and improved treatment for African-Americans in the U.S. military.

Dr. Bethune's legacy as a political powerhouse continues to inspire Black women today. In a recent historic event, Kamala Harris was inaugurated as the first female Vice President of the United States, shattering yet another glass ceiling for women of color. This achievement demonstrates that the barriers Dr. Bethune helped to break down continue to pave the way for future generations of Black women leaders.

In this chapter, we will delve deeper into Dr. Bethune's political prowess, exploring the following key points:

1. Speaking out for justice and using her voice to create change
2. Navigating systems of influence to build political power
3. Championing change through advocacy in action
4. Inspiring future generations with her legacy of leadership

Speaking Out for Justice

Speaking out for justice and using her voice to create change Dr. Mary McLeod Bethune understood the power of her voice and the importance of speaking out for justice. Despite the challenges and discrimination she faced as a Black woman in early 20th-century America, she refused to be silenced. Instead, she utilized her voice to advocate for the rights and needs of her community, ultimately becoming an agent of change.

Dr. Bethune's journey to becoming a fierce advocate began during her childhood. Born to former slaves in South Carolina, she was one of seventeen children. Growing up in the aftermath of the Civil War, her family faced poverty and racial discrimination. However, these hardships only fueled her determination to secure a brighter future for herself and her community.

Education was Dr. Bethune's first step toward using her voice for change. As a young woman, she attended Scotia Seminary in North Carolina and later Moody Bible Institute in Chicago. These experiences not only shaped her intellectually but also provided her with the tools to become an influential leader. Dr. Bethune's passion for education led her to establish a boarding school for Black girls in Daytona Beach, Florida, in 1904. The Daytona Educational and Industrial Training School for Negro Girls started with just six students and grew to become the prestigious Bethune-Cookman College. As an educator, Dr. Bethune understood the importance of empowering young Black women with knowledge and self-confidence. Her school not only provided them with academic opportunities but also instilled a sense of pride and resilience.

As her influence grew, Dr. Bethune leveraged her connections and accomplishments to address the broader issues facing the African-American community. She spoke out against segregation and racial discrimination, advocating for educational and economic opportunities for all Black Americans. Her involvement in various organizations, such as the National Association of Colored Women (NACW) and the National Council of Negro Women (NCNW), allowed her to amplify her voice and work collaboratively with other trailblazing Black women.

Dr. Bethune's commitment to speaking out for justice caught the attention of President Franklin D. Roosevelt, who appointed her as a special advisor on minority affairs in 1935. In this position, she used her voice to champion the needs of African Americans during the Great Depression. As the Director of the NYA's Office of Minority Affairs, Dr. Bethune worked tirelessly to ensure that Black youth had access to the resources and opportunities they needed to thrive. Her advocacy extended beyond the NYA, as she formed and led the Black Cabinet. This group of African-American advisors to President Roosevelt was the first to press for civil rights from within the federal government. Dr. Bethune's voice was crucial in initiating change on a national level. She successfully lobbied for anti-discrimination clauses in government contracts and fought for the integration of the Washington D.C. federal workforce.

Dr. Bethune's legacy as a vocal advocate for justice is a testament to the power of speaking out. She demonstrated that using one's voice can create lasting change and inspire others to join the fight for equality. By standing up against injustice and advocating for her community, Dr. Bethune laid the groundwork for future generations of Black women leaders. Today, we can look to the achievements of trailblazing women like Vice President Kamala Harris as evidence of the lasting impact of Dr. Bethune's advocacy. As the first female Vice President of the United States and the highest-ranking woman of color in U.S. history, Kamala Harris represents the continued progress in the fight for justice and equality.

In this section, we have explored Dr. Bethune's journey to becoming a powerful advocate for justice. From her early days as an educator to her influential role in the to create change and inspire others. Now, let's dive deeper into the lessons we can learn from her experiences and apply them to our own lives.

Political Power: Navigating Systems of Influence

Dr. Mary McLeod Bethune's political acumen and ability to navigate systems of influence enabled her to create lasting change in the lives of African Americans. As a trailblazer and visionary leader, she understood the importance of forging connections and alliances to amplify her message and advance her cause.

One of Dr. Bethune's most significant accomplishments was her work with the National Youth Administration (NYA) and the formation of the Black Cabinet. As the first African-American woman to lead a federal agency, she faced considerable challenges in navigating a political landscape dominated by white men. Yet, Dr. Bethune persevered, using her intelligence, determination, and strategic skills to make a difference.

Her experience with the NYA and the Black Cabinet offers valuable lessons for those who aspire to create change within complex systems of power. Here are some key takeaways from Dr. Bethune's political journey:

1. Build relationships and alliances: Dr. Bethune understood the importance of cultivating relationships with influential individuals and organizations. She formed alliances with key figures, such as First Lady Eleanor Roosevelt, which helped her gain access to resources and opportunities for her community. By forging connections with like-minded individuals and groups, Dr. Bethune was able to amplify her voice and create a more significant impact.
2. Leverage your expertise: Dr. Bethune's background as an educator and her extensive experience working with the African-American community made her a valuable asset to the Roosevelt administration. She used her knowledge and expertise to advocate for policies and programs that would benefit her community. By demonstrating her competence and understanding of the issues, she earned the trust and respect of her colleagues and allies.
3. Be strategic and adaptable: Dr. Bethune was skilled at navigating the complex political landscape of her time. She recognized the need to be strategic and adaptable in her approach, adjusting her tactics and messaging as necessary to achieve her goals. Her ability to adapt and persevere in the face of challenges enabled her to make

significant strides in advancing civil rights and improving the lives of African Americans.

4. Stay true to your values and vision: Despite facing numerous obstacles, Dr. Bethune remained steadfast in her commitment to justice and equality. She never wavered in her belief that education and economic opportunities were the keys to uplifting her community. By staying true to her values and vision, she inspired others to join her in the fight for change.

As we reflect on Dr. Bethune's political prowess and ability to navigate systems of influence, it's essential to consider how we can apply these lessons in our own lives. Whether we're working within a political system, a corporation, or a community organization, these strategies can help us create lasting change and achieve our goals.

In the next section, we will delve into Dr. Bethune's work as an advocate for her community, exploring the ways in which she championed change and inspired others to join her cause.

Advocacy in Action: Championing Change

Throughout her life, Dr. Mary McLeod Bethune was a tireless advocate for her community, using her voice and influence to champion change. As an educator, political leader, and civil rights activist, she fought for the rights and needs of African Americans and paved the way for future generations of Black leaders.

In this section, we will explore some of the key advocacy strategies Dr. Bethune employed in her quest for justice and equality:

- Mobilize and empower your community: Dr. Bethune recognized that lasting change could only be achieved by empowering her community to advocate for their rights and needs. She established organizations such as the National Council of Negro Women (NCNW) to bring together like-minded individuals and provide them with the resources and support they needed to create change. By mobilizing and empowering her community, Dr. Bethune was able to amplify her message and create a more significant impact.
- Collaborate and build coalitions: Dr. Bethune understood that no one person could singlehandedly create change. She actively sought to collaborate with other organizations and form coalitions to advance her cause. By working with allies such as the National Association of Colored Women (NACW) and President Roosevelt's administration, she was able to leverage their collective power to create lasting change for African Americans.
- Raise awareness and educate: As an educator, Dr. Bethune was acutely aware of the power of knowledge and its ability to transform lives. She used her platform to raise awareness about the challenges facing her community and to educate others about the importance of racial equality and justice. Through speeches, writing, and her work with various organizations, she was able to inform and inspire others to join her cause.
- Demonstrate persistence and resilience: Throughout her life, Dr. Bethune faced numerous obstacles and setbacks in her quest for justice. However, she never allowed these challenges to deter her from her mission. Her persistence and resilience in the face of adversity serve as a powerful example for others who seek to create change in their own lives and communities.

By examining Dr. Bethune's advocacy in action, we can learn valuable lessons about how to champion change and create a lasting impact. In the next section, we will explore the legacy of Dr. Bethune's leadership and the ways in which she continues to inspire future generations.

Legacy of Leadership: Inspiring Future Generations

Dr. Mary McLeod Bethune's legacy as a trailblazing leader and advocate for justice continues to inspire future generations of Black women and leaders from all walks of life. Her unwavering commitment to education, civil rights, and the empowerment of her community serves as a powerful reminder of the difference one person can make in the world.

There are several ways in which Dr. Bethune's legacy of leadership continues to inspire and guide others:

1. Role model for resilience and determination: Dr. Bethune's life story is a testament to the power of resilience and determination in the face of adversity. Despite being born to former slaves and facing numerous challenges throughout her life, she rose to become an influential leader and change-maker. Her story serves as a powerful reminder that with hard work, determination, and a clear vision, we can overcome obstacles and achieve greatness.
2. Mentorship and guidance: Dr. Bethune's work as an educator and mentor to countless young Black women helped shape the next generation of leaders. By providing guidance and support to those who followed in her footsteps, she created a ripple effect that continues to be felt today.
3. Commitment to social justice and equality: Dr. Bethune's unwavering commitment to social justice and equality

serves as a guiding light for those who seek to create change in their own communities. Her tireless efforts to fight for the rights and needs of African Americans demonstrate the importance of standing up for what is right and using our voices to advocate for those who are marginalized.

4. Leadership by example: As a pioneering leader in both education and politics, Dr. Bethune led by example, showing others what was possible when one remains true to their values and vision. Her accomplishments and the impact she made on the lives of countless individuals serve as a powerful reminder of the importance of stepping up and taking charge when the opportunity arises.

As we reflect on the legacy of Dr. Mary McLeod Bethune's leadership, we are reminded of the power and potential that lies within each of us to create change and make a difference in the world. By embracing the lessons and wisdom of Dr. Bethune's life, we can find the inspiration and guidance we need to forge our own path toward greatness.

As we conclude our exploration of Dr. Mary McLeod Bethune's life and legacy, let's consider how we can apply the transformative lessons she left behind to our own lives. Here are some key takeaways and strategies for personal growth and empowerment:

1. Embrace your unique voice and use it for change: Like Dr. Bethune, recognize the power of your own voice and the importance of using it to advocate for justice and equality. Speak out against discrimination and injustice and use your platform to raise awareness and inspire others to join your cause.

2. Invest in your own education and personal growth: Dr. Bethune's commitment to education and lifelong learning allowed her to overcome obstacles and achieve greatness. Embrace a similar mindset by seeking out opportunities for learning and growth, whether it's through formal education, mentorship, or personal development programs.

3. Surround yourself with supportive allies and mentors: Dr. Bethune's success was due in part to the relationships and alliances she forged with like-minded individuals and organizations. Cultivate your own network of support, seeking out mentors and allies who share your values and can provide guidance and encouragement along your journey.

4. Persevere in the face of adversity: As Dr. Bethune's life demonstrates, resilience and determination are key to overcoming challenges and achieving success. Embrace a mindset of persistence and never give up on your dreams and goals, no matter the obstacles you may face. By incorporating these lessons and strategies into our own lives, we can draw strength and inspiration from Dr. Bethune's remarkable legacy. As we embark on our journey to self-discovery and empowerment, let's remember the transformative power of Dr. Mary McLeod Bethune's life and teachings, using her wisdom as a blueprint for our own path to greatness.

5. Harness the power of unity and sisterhood: Dr. Bethune recognized the importance of collaboration and unity in the fight for equality and justice. As you pursue your own goals, look for opportunities to join forces with others who share your values and vision. Cultivating a sense of sisterhood and camaraderie can make you stronger and more effective in your efforts.

Now that we've explored Dr. Mary McLeod Bethune's life and the transformative lessons she left behind, let's take a moment to reflect on some action steps we can take to embody her wisdom and apply it to our own lives:

Action Step 1: Reflect on your own voice and the causes that are important to you. Identify ways you can use your voice to advocate for change, whether it's through writing, speaking, or organizing events and campaigns.

Action Step 2: Set aside time each week for learning and personal development. This could include reading books, attending workshops or seminars, or engaging in online courses. Embrace a mindset of curiosity and growth and be open to new ideas and perspectives.

Action Step 3: Seek out mentors and allies who can support and guide you on your journey. Attend networking events, join professional organizations, or reach out to individuals who inspire you. Cultivate relationships with those who share your values and can provide valuable advice and encouragement.

Action Step 4: Develop a personal resilience plan to help you navigate challenges and setbacks. This could include strategies for managing stress, staying motivated, and maintaining a positive mindset, even in the face of adversity.

Action Step 5: Look for opportunities to collaborate with others in your community or industry. Join clubs, organizations, or online groups where you can connect with like-minded individuals and work together to create positive change.

By incorporating these action steps into our lives, we can begin to harness the transformative power of Dr. Mary McLeod Bethune's legacy and make a lasting impact on the world around us. As we continue on our journey to self-discovery and empowerment, let us always remember the strength, resilience, and wisdom of Dr. Bethune, and strive to embody her unwavering determination to make a difference in the lives of others.

A Timeless Legacy: Empowering Future Generations

As we delve into the final section of this chapter, let us consider the lasting impact of Dr. Mary McLeod Bethune's legacy on future generations. Her life's work, which centered on education, civil rights, and the empowerment of Black women, continues to inspire and influence countless individuals today. By learning from her example, we can carry the torch of her legacy and empower ourselves and future generations to rise above adversity and achieve greatness.

Dr. Bethune's life serves as a testament to the power of resilience and determination in overcoming barriers and breaking through societal limitations. Her unwavering commitment to the advancement of Black women and her belief in the transformative power of education continue to resonate with us today. By honoring her legacy, we not only pay tribute to her extraordinary accomplishments but also ensure that her message of hope, perseverance, and empowerment is carried forward for generations to come.

Here are some key ways in which we can honor Dr. Bethune's legacy and empower future generations:

1. Advocate for educational opportunities: Just as Dr. Bethune championed education as a means to empowerment, we must continue to fight for equal access to quality education for all. By supporting initiatives and organizations that promote educational equity, we can help ensure that future generations have the tools and resources they need to thrive.

2. Encourage mentorship and intergenerational connections: Dr. Bethune's life was enriched by the relationships she forged with both mentors and mentees. By fostering connections between different generations, we can help create a powerful network of support, knowledge, and experience that can uplift and empower those who come after us.

3. Promote representation and inclusivity: Dr. Bethune's groundbreaking work in politics and civil rights helped pave the way for greater representation of Black women in positions of power and influence. We must continue to advocate for diverse voices and perspectives in all areas of society, from politics and media to education and the workplace.

4. Foster a spirit of resilience and determination: As we face challenges and obstacles in our own lives, let us draw strength from Dr. Bethune's unwavering determination and refusal to accept defeat. By cultivating a resilient mindset and passing it on to future generations, we can inspire others to persevere in the face of adversity and strive for greatness.

In conclusion, the legacy of Dr. Mary McLeod Bethune offers us a blueprint for personal growth, empowerment, and transformation. As we embark on our own journey of self-discovery, let us honor her memory by embodying the lessons and wisdom she left behind. By doing so, we not only pay tribute to her extraordinary life but also ensure that her message of hope, perseverance, and empowerment is carried forward for generations to come.

May the timeless legacy of Dr. Mary McLeod Bethune inspire and guide us on our path to greatness, and may her spirit of resilience, determination, and advocacy for justice and equality continue to illuminate our way.

7 Affirmations for this Chapter

1. I am a powerful advocate for justice and equality, following in the footsteps of Dr. Mary McLeod Bethune.
2. My voice matters, and I use it to speak out against injustice and uplift my community.
3. I am inspired by Dr. Bethune's determination and resilience, and I embody these qualities in my own journey.
4. I actively seek opportunities to learn from the wisdom of trailblazing Black women, drawing strength and purpose from their stories.
5. I am an agent of change, using my influence to create a more inclusive and equitable world for future generations.
6. I honor the legacy of Dr. Mary McLeod Bethune by embracing my authentic self and living a life of greatness.
7. I am connected to a powerful sisterhood of Black women, united in our mission to transform the world and empower one another.

TOGETHER, WE ARE STRONGER
DrEvelyn

Chapter 7

The Power of Faith, Vision, and Education

In a time when the possibilities for African American women were brutally limited, there emerged an undeterred soul, Mary Jane McLeod Bethune, whose journey in life demonstrated not just her exceptional tenacity but also her boundless faith in God's plan and the transformative power of education.

Born as the first free child in a large family that had tasted the bitter pill of enslavement, Mary stood out. Her likes and dislikes, her way of thinking, it was all distinct. At the tender age of 6 or 7, she had an experience that profoundly shaped her destiny. During a visit with her mother Patsy at work, a harsh truth was thrown at her. A white child, seeing her pick up a book, snatched it away, telling her, "Put that book down. You can't read and write!" This incident, rather than discouraging her, ignited a spark within. She made a solemn vow to herself and to God - she would learn to read and write.

And learn she did. When a Protestant Missionary came to the fields announcing the opening of a school for the children of the plantation, Mary was the one chosen from her family to attend. She walked the long miles to and from school each day, never daunted, because this was the path she had prayed for. As her education unfolded, Mary didn't keep it to herself. She shared her knowledge, teaching her parents and others in her community to read and write.

The promise of that young girl grew into the unshakeable faith of a woman who knew, deep within her soul, that her mission in life was larger than herself. It was about being a voice for the voiceless, about guiding her people to discover their dignity through education.

Driven by her philosophy of "Enter to Learn and Depart to Serve," Dr. Bethune grew her innate talents and skills to be a woman of extraordinary influence, standing shoulder to shoulder with giants of her time like Eleanor Roosevelt. This friendship opened doors to resources and opportunities for an underserved and discriminated population. Her leadership paved the way for the integration of the military, from the Women's Army Corps to the funding of the Tuskegee Airmen. Her contributions were so significant that they found a place in the history of the military and the Congressional Record.

When we reflect on Dr. Bethune's life, there are elements that stand out - her unflinching faith in God's plan, her conviction in education as a tool for freedom, and her relentless pursuit of excellence in every task she undertook, no matter how big or small.

As we embark on this chapter, let's bring Dr. Bethune's legacy into the current times. Consider Shonda Rhimes' impact on television and storytelling. Like Dr. Bethune, Rhimes dared to tread a path less trodden, crafting narratives that echo with diverse voices, breaking barriers, and redefining norms.

Throughout this chapter, we will delve into the following themes:

- Section 1: Core Commitments: Discovering Your Values
- Section 2: Purposeful Passion: Aligning Actions with Intentions
- Section 3: Guiding Grace: Cultivating Spiritual Resilience
- Section 4: Unyielding Uniqueness: Embracing Authenticity

Dr. Bethune's life story serves as a guide for us to explore these themes. Let's proceed, inspired by her courage, determination, and faith.

Core Commitments: Discovering Your Values

To understand the essence of core commitments, let's delve deeper into the life of Mary McLeod Bethune. Dr. Bethune's core values were rooted in faith, education, service, and excellence. Her dedication to these tenets directed her path and catalyzed her success as an influential civil rights activist and educator.

Faith was the cornerstone of her beliefs. As the daughter of former slaves, the odds were stacked against her, but it was her unwavering faith that bolstered her spirit. She believed in divine guidance and held fast to the belief that God had a specific plan for her, which was to uplift and educate her community.

Education held a special place in Dr. Bethune's values. As someone who thirsted for knowledge from a young age, she saw education as the ticket to freedom, a tool for empowerment, and a means to break free from the shackles of oppression and marginalization. She didn't keep this belief to herself; she worked tirelessly to ensure that others, especially the African-American community, had access to quality education.

Service was another cornerstone of her values. Dr. Bethune believed in serving her community. The phrase "Enter to Learn and Depart to Serve" was not just a motto but a guiding principle in her life. She dedicated her life to serving others, a testament to her selflessness and commitment to the betterment of society.

Finally, excellence was a value she upheld and promoted. Regardless of the task's magnitude, she was a firm believer in doing it to the best of her abilities, demonstrating a commitment to excellence that's inspiring to all. Let's now draw a parallel to a contemporary influential Black woman, Joy-Ann Reid. Joy, an accomplished television host and national correspondent for MSNBC showcases her core values of integrity, professionalism, and justice in her work. Like Dr. Bethune, Joy is deeply committed to her values and uses her platform to influence and inform her audience.

Integrity is a core value that Joy consistently upholds in her journalistic work. She values truth and is committed to presenting her audience with factual, unbiased news. In an era where fake news and misinformation can easily spread, Joy's dedication to integrity is not just commendable but necessary.

Professionalism is another core value she embodies. As a Black woman in a predominately white industry, she faces unique challenges and hurdles. Despite these, she carries herself with poise and professionalism, always prepared, always diligent, and consistently delivering high-quality work. Finally, justice is a value that Joy passionately believes in. She uses her platform to shed light on social justice issues, amplifying marginalized voices and challenging systemic injustices. She is a strong advocate for racial and social equality, consistently using her influence to push for change.

In comparing the lives of Dr. Bethune and Joy Reid, we see how both women allowed their core values to guide their paths. The values they embraced empowered them to make significant impacts in their respective fields. The key to their success lies in their unwavering commitment to their values and their dedication to aligning their actions with those values.

As we progress through this chapter, consider what values guide you. What principles do you hold dear, and how do they influence your life and decisions? The understanding and alignment with these core values is what makes trailblazers like Dr. Bethune and Joy Reid not just successful, but influential and impactful. Reflect on these values as we move into the next section, where we will explore aligning your actions with your intentions.

Core Commitments: Discovering Your Values

Dr. Mary McLeod Bethune exemplified how steadfast commitment to core values serves as a compass, guiding our decisions and actions toward a meaningful, fulfilling life. Bethune, born into a world that undervalued and underprivileged her, lived by a set of core values that became the foundation for her remarkable achievements. Those core values were poured into her by her family, her father and mother, and her community.

The core value she held closest was education; Bethune considered it a means to freedom and the key to a prosperous life. Her strong conviction that knowledge was power guided her to establish the Daytona Educational and Industrial Training School for Negro Girls, which later became Bethune-Cookman College. The institution, borne out of her belief in education, continues to uphold this value by providing access to quality education for countless individuals.

Another of Bethune's core commitments was equality. A staunch advocate for racial and gender equality, she didn't merely believe in these principles - she lived them. She championed causes that furthered these values, participating in the foundation of organizations such as the National Council of Negro Women and advocating for national policy changes.

Faith played an integral role in Bethune's life and formed another of her core values. Her unwavering faith gave her the courage and determination to accomplish her ambitious goals. Her belief in divine guidance is evident in the prayer she wrote for her college, where she sought wisdom, courage, and a heart that refused to hate.

In contemporary society, there are individuals who mirror Bethune's core commitments in their fields of influence. One such individual is Joy-Ann Reid, a national correspondent for MSNBC. A powerhouse in the world of media, Reid showcases a commitment to education through her articulate commentary on complex sociopolitical issues, providing valuable insights to her audience and fostering an educated public.

Reid, like Bethune, holds equality as a non-negotiable. She uses her platform to shine a spotlight on issues of racial and gender inequality, consistently advocating for fairness and justice. Reid, through her thoughtful dialogue and steadfast refusal to allow inequality to go unchallenged, carries forward Bethune's legacy of commitment to equality.

Finally, Reid, in the face of immense challenges and backlash in her career, has exhibited remarkable resilience and determination, hinting at a strong faith mirroring Bethune's. Her steadfastness in expressing her truth, regardless of the obstacles in her path, is a testament to her unyielding faith in her mission.

Dr. Bethune and Joy-Ann Reid exemplify the transformative power of core commitments. Their lives demonstrate how discovering and living by our values can chart a path toward personal and societal advancement. They provide us with a model of how to align our actions with our values, inspiring us to follow their trailblazing paths.

In summary, the essence of Dr. Mary McLeod Bethune's life teaches us to find our core commitments and hold on to them as we navigate our unique journeys. Whether it be education, equality, faith, or any other value that resonates with us, let's commit to live it out, just as Bethune and Reid have. These women, through their dedication to their core values, remind us of the power that resides within each of us, waiting to be unleashed.

Guiding Grace: Cultivating Spiritual Resilience

Just as Mary McLeod Bethune and Joy Reid had their core values, they also relied on their spiritual resilience, a strength that comes from a place deep within, to guide them through life's trials and triumphs. Their stories illustrate the power of spiritual resilience in overcoming adversities and achieving success.

In Mary McLeod Bethune's case, spiritual resilience took the form of her unwavering faith. Born just after the end of the American Civil War, the path toward her destiny was not smooth. Yet, in every hardship, she found strength in her faith, and her belief in God directing her path. Her faith gave her the willpower to endure, the courage to persevere, and the strength to overcome obstacles in her path. From fighting for education in a deeply segregated society to creating opportunities for marginalized communities, her spiritual resilience was a shining beacon that led the way.

Her faith wasn't just a source of personal strength; it was a tool she used to inspire others. By standing strong in her beliefs and principles, she fostered hope in the people around her, making her not just a leader, but a beacon of inspiration for generations.

Fast forward to the present, and we can see the same spiritual resilience in Joy Reid. In navigating the volatile landscape of journalism and media, Joy has faced significant challenges and adversities. From dealing with professional setbacks to facing public criticism, her journey has not been easy. Yet, she remains steadfast and resilient, anchored by her belief in truth, justice, and the power of information.

Her spiritual resilience manifests in her commitment to her work, in her dedication to truth, and in her determination to utilize her platform for positive change. Despite the backlash and criticism that often come with her job, she maintains her grace and composure, standing firm in her principles and continuing to use her voice for the greater good.

These women serve as powerful examples of how spiritual resilience can guide us in our path, providing us with the strength and grace to navigate life's challenges. Their stories remind us that spiritual resilience is not about avoiding hardships but facing them with courage, fortitude, and an unyielding faith in our values and beliefs.

As you continue on your journey, remember that cultivating spiritual resilience is an essential part of trailblazing your path. Like Dr. Bethune and Joy Reid, you too can draw strength from your beliefs and values, using them as your guiding light in times of adversity. As we move forward, let's explore how embracing authenticity, another trailblazing tenet can further empower us to define our path.

Unyielding Uniqueness: Embracing Authenticity

One of the most compelling facets of Dr. Mary McLeod Bethune's life is her unyielding uniqueness. In an era when conformity was often a survival strategy for African Americans, Bethune dared to embrace her authenticity. She harnessed her distinctive qualities - her courage, her resilience, her vision - to confront the status quo and create transformative change.

Dr. Bethune's most audacious act of authenticity was founding a school for African-American girls at a time when they were systematically denied the right to education. She didn't just recognize the injustice; she refused to accept it. In her unique way, Bethune blended her role as an educator with activism, turning her school into a bastion of resistance against racial inequality.

Just as Dr. Bethune's unyielding uniqueness shaped her path, today's trailblazers are also tapping into their authenticity. Take, for example, Ava DuVernay, an acclaimed filmmaker, and producer. DuVernay didn't conform to Hollywood's norms and expectations. Instead, she carved out her own space, producing powerful narratives that spotlight underrepresented groups and experiences. Her groundbreaking work, including the award-winning film "Selma" and the Netflix miniseries "When They See Us," brought to the fore stories that were overlooked or misconstrued in mainstream media.

Like Bethune, DuVernay's authenticity doesn't stop at her work; it extends to her activism. She's used her platform to shine a light on racial injustice, mass incarceration, and other critical issues, constantly pushing the boundaries of what's expected of a Hollywood filmmaker.

As DuVernay and Bethune have shown us, our unyielding uniqueness is an asset, not a liability. It is what allows us to stand out, to innovate, to see possibilities where others see roadblocks. Our authenticity imbues our work and our lives with a depth and richness that cannot be replicated.

Embracing our authenticity is not always easy. We may fear rejection or judgment, or we may feel pressure to fit into a pre-established mold. But as we strive to define our paths, it is crucial that we remain true to who we are. Authenticity is the compass that can guide us when the way forward is unclear. It is the source of our resilience and creativity, the bedrock of our integrity.

In the end, our unyielding uniqueness is our ultimate power. It enables us to make our mark, to influence change, and to contribute to the world in ways that only we can. As we draw inspiration from trailblazers like Dr. Bethune and Ava DuVernay, let us honor and harness our authenticity, remembering that our unyielding uniqueness is not only our right but our gift to the world.

In the final section of this chapter, we'll bring these principles together, considering how we can apply these tenets in our lives and set forth on our unique paths.

Bringing It All Together: Defining Your Unique Path

So, we have been on a remarkable journey, examining the tenets that guided the extraordinary life of Dr. Mary McLeod Bethune, and how they resonate with the lives of trailblazing Black women today. We have explored core commitments, purposeful passion, guiding grace, and unyielding uniqueness. Now, the question stands, how can we apply these tenets to our own lives? How can we define our unique path and become trailblazers in our own right?

In exploring Dr. Bethune's life, we saw that she was driven by a strong commitment to her core values. She understood that these values were not just abstract concepts, but guiding principles that informed every decision she made and every step she took. In our lives, we too must identify our core values and let them guide our actions. Whether it's a commitment to justice, a passion for education, or a dedication to serving our communities, these values form the foundation of our unique path.

Next, we delved into the concept of purposeful passion. We saw that Dr. Bethune's passion for education was not a vague sentiment but a driving force that propelled her to establish a school and break down barriers. Like Dr. Bethune and Joy Reid, we too must recognize our passions and act on them. Our passions are not merely hobbies or interests; they are the sparks that can ignite change and make a difference in the world.

We also explored guiding grace, looking at how Dr. Bethune's faith gave her the resilience to overcome obstacles and challenges. Like her, we must cultivate spiritual resilience, finding our source of inner strength and peace. Whether it comes from religious faith, meditation, connection with nature, or personal relationships, this guiding grace can sustain us in times of difficulty and uncertainty.

Finally, we examined unyielding uniqueness, celebrating the authenticity of trailblazers like Dr. Bethune and Ava DuVernay. We understood that our uniqueness is our strength, not our weakness. It is our source of innovation, creativity, and integrity. As we define our unique path, we must embrace our authenticity, recognizing that our individuality is a gift to the world.

In conclusion, defining our unique path requires us to embrace our core values, to act with purposeful passion, to cultivate spiritual resilience, and to honor our authenticity. It is a journey of self-discovery, courage, and commitment. It is a journey that demands we honor the trailblazers who came before us and become trailblazers for those who will follow. As we venture forth, let us hold fast to the tenets that guided Dr. Mary McLeod Bethune, daring to dream, to act, and to make a difference.

Remember, the path you are defining is uniquely yours, trailblazed by the imprint of your footprints. Keep walking, keep striving, and keep making a difference in this world. It's time to define your path and become the trailblazer you were born to be.

7 Affirmations to Lift, Empower and Encourage

1. "I embrace the wisdom and strength of trailblazing women like Dr. Mary McLeod Bethune, drawing inspiration from their journeys to guide my own path to greatness."
2. "My core commitments and authentic self serve as my guiding light, empowering me to make a meaningful impact in my life and the lives of others."
3. "I align my actions with my intentions and core values, knowing that this unwavering commitment will propel me towards my personal and professional goals."
4. "With grace and resilience, I overcome challenges and setbacks, trusting that each experience is an opportunity for growth and self-discovery."
5. "I honor the legacy of trailblazing Black women by actively seeking inspiration from their stories, using their experiences to fuel my own journey towards greatness."
6. "By cultivating spiritual resilience and embracing gratitude, I remain grounded and focused on my purpose, even in the face of adversity."
7. "I am a powerful, unique, and authentic individual, and by honoring my true self, I will make a lasting impact on the world around me."

Imagine - Knowledge Expands Your Horizons
DrEvelyn

Chapter 8

Radiant Resurgence: Reclaiming Your Power

My dear sisters and brothers, I invite you to journey back in time with me, to the turn of the 20th century, where we find a woman of extraordinary resilience, Dr. Mary McLeod Bethune. Let her life be a testament to the fact that no matter what odds we face, we can rise, we can shine, we can thrive.

Dr. Bethune was born just a few years after the abolition of slavery, the fifteenth child of former slaves, Samuel and Patsy McLeod. Despite the shackles of societal discrimination and the limitations of poverty, she was determined to get an education. Through sheer will and a spirit that refused to be broken, she became a teacher, dedicating her life to the upliftment of her people. But she wasn't content with just uplifting herself. No, she had a grand vision.

In 1904, Dr. Bethune founded the Daytona Literary and Industrial Training School for Negro Girls in Florida. Now, imagine my sister, the hurdles she must have faced in a time when the state of Florida spent $11.50 per year on the education of white children and a mere $2.64 per year on black children. Yet, she persevered. She opened her school with six students, five girls, and her son Albert.

Despite the vast chasm of inequality, Dr. Bethune understood the power of education, the power of her voice, and the power of the ballot box. She realized that the decisions that affected her and her people were made by elected officials who catered to their constituencies, and those constituencies did not include African-Americans. In creating her school, she was determined to address the needs of African-American girls, to give them the tools to shape their own destinies.

Now, let's connect Dr. Bethune's story to a more recent one, that of Serena Williams. Serena, like Dr. Bethune, faced immense obstacles in her journey. After her pregnancy, she suffered serious health complications that threatened her career. But Serena, the champion that she is, bounced back. She returned to the tennis court, stronger, more determined, and inspired millions of women worldwide with her resilience.

The promise for you, my dear sister, lies in the lessons we can learn from these extraordinary women. From Dr. Bethune, we learn the power of resilience, the power of vision, and the power of action. From Serena, we learn that no setback is too great to overcome.

In this chapter, we will explore :

- Overcoming Obstacles: Bouncing Back Stronger
- Rediscovering Resolve: Nurturing Perseverance
- Stepping into Self-Love: Embracing Your Worth

· Triumph in Transformation: Harnessing Inner Strength

This journey won't be easy, but remember, you are not alone. You stand on the shoulders of giants, women who have faced and overcome adversity. You, too, can reclaim your power.

Overcoming Obstacles: Bouncing Back Stronger

Sister, hear me when I say that your setbacks are not your final destination. They are merely opportunities to grow, to rise above, to become more than you ever thought possible. Dr. Bethune and Serena Williams are testaments to this truth. But how can we apply their lessons to our own lives? Let's explore together.

Embrace Adversity as a Catalyst for Growth

When Dr. Bethune encountered a roadblock, she didn't shy away or accept defeat. Instead, she used it as a catalyst to propel her forward. Understand that adversity isn't meant to destroy you; it is an opportunity to build strength and character.

Take a moment to reflect on the obstacles in your life. Consider how they have shaped you, how they have made you wiser, more resilient. Embrace them, my sister, and let them fuel your growth.

Keep Your Eyes on the Prize

Dr. Bethune and Serena Williams both had an unwavering focus on their goals. Whether it was building a school or re-turning to the tennis court, they never lost sight of what they wanted to achieve. Identify your goals, your dreams, and your aspirations. Write them down, and keep them at the forefront of your mind. When the path becomes difficult, remember why you started. This clarity of purpose will help you push through any challenge that comes your way.

Surround Yourself with a Supportive Circle

Our journey to greatness is not meant to be a solitary one. We are not islands, but interconnected beings who thrive on the love and support of others. Dr. Bethune built her school with the help of her community, and Serena Williams leaned on her family and friends during her recovery. Surround yourself with people who believe in you, who lift you up, and who share your vision. Together, you can overcome any obstacle and achieve incredible heights.

Never Give Up

Both Dr. Bethune and Serena Williams faced immense challenges, but they never gave up. They fought with every ounce of their being, pushing through pain and adversity to achieve their goals. Remember, my sister, that the road to greatness is paved with obstacles. When you encounter them, don't back down. Don't give up. Keep pushing forward, for you are made of the same stuff as these incredible women, and you, too, can overcome.

Rediscovering Resolve: Nurturing Perseverance

As we turn to the next part of our journey together, I want you to think about the quality that underpins resilience: perseverance. It was perseverance that enabled Dr. Bethune to open her school against all odds. It was perseverance that allowed Serena Williams to return to her sport and perform at a high level after childbirth and severe health complications.

Let's delve into how you can nurture this essential trait within yourself.

Perseverance isn't born overnight. It's a quality that's cultivated over time, through patience and steadfastness. Dr. Bethune didn't establish her school in a day or even a year. She met with many roadblocks, faced numerous disappointments, but she held fast to her vision, patiently working towards it day by day. Developing patience and steadfastness begins with accepting that progress can be slow, and setbacks are normal. It requires an unwavering commitment to your vision, even when progress seems elusive.

Our minds are powerful tools that can either lift us up or pull us down. When we feed our minds with positivity, we strengthen our ability to persevere. Serena Williams, even in the face of harsh criticism and physical challenges, maintained a positive outlook, focusing on her recovery and return to tennis.

Cultivate a habit of positive self-talk. Surround yourself with uplifting messages and people. When you encounter obstacles, remember to keep a hopeful perspective. Challenges are not roadblocks on your path to success; they are stepping stones. Each challenge you encounter holds valuable lessons that can help you grow and move closer to your goals. Dr. Bethune viewed the challenges she faced as opportunities to learn and become a better leader.

When faced with a challenge, shift your perspective. Ask yourself, "What can I learn from this?" Embrace the opportunity to grow and come out stronger on the other side. Perseverance doesn't mean pushing yourself to the brink of exhaustion. It involves understanding your limits and treating yourself with compassion. Serena Williams took the time she needed to heal and recover before returning to her sport. She knew that her health and well-being were paramount.

Practice self-compassion. It's okay to rest when you're tired, to take a break when you need it. Remember, you're not in a race. Your journey to greatness is a marathon, not a sprint. In nurturing perseverance, remember that the journey is just as important as the destination. Every step you take, no matter how small, is a step towards your goals. As you cultivate patience, feed your mind with positivity, embrace challenges, and practice self-compassion, you're building the foundation of perseverance that will serve you in all areas of your life.

Stepping into Self-Love: Embracing Your Worth

In this part of our journey, we will explore the concept of self-love and its role in reclaiming your power. Dr. Bethune was a woman of profound faith, and this faith informed her sense of self-love and worth. Despite the adversities she faced, she never allowed her circumstances to define her value. Dr. Bethune was a woman deeply rooted in her faith. She believed that she, like every human being, was created in the image of God, and this belief shaped her understanding of her own worth. She saw herself not as a victim of her circumstances but as a child of God, endowed with inherent value and potential.

This is where self-love begins - in recognizing your divine worth. You are not your failures, your setbacks, or your struggles. You are a unique and valuable individual, deserving of love and respect. Faith played a crucial role in Dr. Bethune's life. It was her faith that gave her the strength to face adversity, to persevere when the odds were against her, and to love herself even when society tried to tell her she was less than. Faith can serve as a foundation for self-love, providing a constant reminder of your worth and potential.

Cultivate your faith, whatever form it may take. Let it ground you in your journey of self-love and be a source of strength and comfort in times of adversity. Self-love involves more than just recognizing your worth. It also entails taking care of yourself - physically, mentally, and spiritually. Dr. Bethune understood this. Despite her many responsibilities, she made time for prayer and reflection, understanding that caring for her spiritual health was as important as any other task.

Self-care is an act of self-love. It's about setting boundaries, taking time to rest and rejuvenate, and prioritizing your well-being. Treat yourself with kindness and compassion, just as you would a loved one. Affirmations can be a powerful tool for cultivating self-love. Dr. Bethune used her faith-based affirmations to remind herself of her worth and to inspire her to pursue her goals despite the obstacles she faced. Create your own set of affirmations that resonate with you. Speak them aloud every day. Remind yourself that you are loved, you are worthy, and you are capable of achieving your dreams.

Embracing self-love is a vital step in reclaiming your power. By recognizing your divine worth, cultivating faith, practicing self-care, and affirming your worth, you are creating a foundation of self-love that will empower you to overcome adversity and achieve your dreams.

Triumph in Transformation: Harnessing Inner Strength

Our journey now leads us to the power of transformation. As we've seen in the life of Dr. Bethune, transformation isn't just about external changes. It's about the internal shift in mindset, attitudes, and beliefs. It's about harnessing your inner strength to rise above your circumstances and actualize your potential.

Change, while often daunting, is a necessary part of life and personal growth. Dr. Bethune navigated numerous changes throughout her life, from her humble beginnings to founding her school and becoming an influential leader. She embraced these changes, viewing them not as threats but as opportunities for growth. Embrace change in your life. Whether it's a new job, a new city, or a new phase of life, see it as an opportunity to grow, learn, and evolve.

Dr. Bethune was born in a time when society had set limitations on what she, as a black woman, could aspire to. But she refused to be confined by these societal beliefs. She believed in her potential and dared to challenge the status quo.

Identify and challenge any limiting beliefs you may hold about yourself. Remember that you are capable of more than you think. Don't let self-doubt or societal expectations hinder your progress.

In every challenge she faced, Dr. Bethune called upon her inner strength. It was this strength that helped her overcome obstacles, endure hardships, and achieve her goals. Your inner strength is your most potent resource. It's the power that can propel you towards your dreams. Harness your inner strength. Tap into your courage, resilience, and determination. Remember that you have overcome challenges before, and you have the strength to overcome whatever lies ahead.

A growth mindset is the belief that abilities and intelligence can be developed through dedication and hard work. Dr. Bethune embodied this mindset. Despite her difficult circumstances, she believed in her ability to learn, grow, and achieve her goals. Cultivate a growth mindset. Embrace challenges as opportunities for learning. Persevere in the face of setbacks. Believe in your ability to grow and evolve.

Transformation is not a destination but a journey. It's about continuously learning, growing, and evolving. As you embrace change, challenge limiting beliefs, harness your inner strength, and cultivate a growth mindset, you'll find yourself on a path of transformation leading to your true potential.

Harnessing the Power of Resilience

Throughout this chapter, we have journeyed through the life of Dr. Mary McLeod Bethune, learning valuable lessons on resilience, faith, self-love, and transformation. The strength of her character, the depth of her faith, the power of her self-love, and the magnitude of her transformation serve as potent reminders of what we can achieve when we harness our inner strength. Dr. Bethune's life was a testament to the power of resilience. Despite the obstacles and setbacks, she remained steadfast in her mission, her faith providing a firm foundation. From her, we learn that resilience is not merely about weathering the storm, but about learning to dance in the rain. It's about finding the strength within us to rise, time and again, stronger and wiser.

We learned the importance of self-love and embracing our worth. Dr. Bethune's faith played an integral role in her sense of self-love and self-worth. She saw herself not as a victim of her circumstances, but as a valuable individual deserving of respect and dignity. This recognition of her worth enabled her to reclaim her power and shape her destiny.

Lastly, we delved into the power of transformation. Dr. Bethune's life was a vivid illustration of how harnessing inner strength can lead to profound transformation. She challenged limiting beliefs, embraced change, and cultivated a growth mindset, leading her to achieve her goals and leave a lasting legacy.

ACTION STEPS:

Reflect on your resilience: Think about the challenges you've overcome in the past and the strengths you've developed as a result. Use this as a source of encouragement for future obstacles.

Cultivate self-love: Make time each day for self-care activities that nourish your mind, body, and spirit. Speak affirmations that remind you of your worth.

Embrace change: View changes in your life as opportunities for growth rather than threats. Adapt and evolve with these changes.

Challenge limiting beliefs: Identify any beliefs that may be holding you back and confront them. Remember, you are capable of more than you think.

Cultivate a growth mindset: Embrace challenges as opportunities for learning. Persevere in the face of setbacks, and believe in your ability to grow and evolve.

Dr. Mary McLeod Bethune was a beacon of resilience, a testament to the power of faith, an embodiment of self-love, and an icon of transformative power. Her life's journey offers timeless wisdom for our journeys of personal growth and empowerment.

Let her story inspire you, her faith strengthen you, her self-love nurture you, and her transformation empower you. Remember, the power to transform your life lies within you.

Embrace it, harness it, and let it lead you to your destiny of greatness.

7 Affirmations for this chapter

1. "I am deeply connected to my roots, drawing strength from the courageous Black women who have come before me."
2. "Every challenge I face is an opportunity for transformation, mirroring the perseverance of Dr. Mary McLeod Bethune."
3. "Just as Dr. Bethune did, I possess the power to change my world and impact my community positively."
4. "Inspired by the legacy of Dr. Bethune, I have the ability to reach my highest potential and achieve greatness."
5. "I am a trailblazer in my own right, paving the way for future generations just as Dr. Bethune did."
6. "In the face of adversity, I am resilient. I rise, just as Dr. Bethune did, rooted in my faith and purpose."
7. "Through self-love and acknowledgment of my worth, I am empowered to create my own legacy, inspired by the life of   Dr. Mary McLeod Bethune."

We Are READY TO GO!
DrEvelyn

Chapter 9

Visionary Vibrance: Imagining a Brighter Future

There was a force, a light, that emanated from the soul of Mary McLeod Bethune. It was the light of a beacon, guiding ships lost in a sea of despair and ignorance toward the shore of knowledge and hope. Born to parents who had known the chains of slavery, Dr. Bethune would rise to become an educator, a civil rights leader, and a beacon of hope for millions of African Americans.

Dr. Bethune faced an immense problem: the entrenched stereotypes and systemic racism that pervaded American society in her time. This was not just a matter of the Negro's own thinking, as she pointed out. The real challenge lay in shifting the stereotyped, nervous thinking of the world's non-colored minority. Yet, the so-called "Negro problem," as it was termed, did not faze her. She was not one to be dragged down by such a weight.

Instead, she found a solution in education. Understanding the power that knowledge could wield, she founded the Daytona Educational and Industrial School for Negro Girls in 1904. A single dollar and fifty cents, a faith as deep as the ocean, and an unyielding belief in the potential of her people were her starting capital. In the face of almost insurmountable obstacles, she built an institution that would become a monument to the possibilities of education and the power of belief.

In her own words, Dr. Bethune once said, "The whole world opened to me when I learned to read." This woman, who would become a towering figure in American history, started her journey in a humble mission school for black children. It was here, in the crucible of education, that Dr. Bethune shaped her vision for a brighter future. She held the belief that, under God's guidance in this great democracy, the Negro race could rise out of the darkness of slavery into the light of freedom.

Fast forward to our current era, and we see the same spirit of resilience and determination embodied in many influential women. Consider Greta Thunberg, a young woman who, despite her tender age, has taken up the mantle of climate activism. She has faced down world leaders and criticized inaction in the face of the looming climate crisis. Her dedication to her cause mirrors Dr. Bethune's commitment to education and civil rights. Both women, despite the odds, dared to dream and take action to make a difference.

In this chapter, we will journey through the visionary vibrance of imagining a brighter future. We will explore four key elements that light our path toward this future.

Section 1: "Dreaming and Doing: Envisioning Possibilities," where we explore the power of dreams and the courage to act on them.

Section 2: "Hope as a Catalyst: Inspiring Change," where we delve into the role of hope in sparking transformative change.

Section 3: "Future-Focused: Planning for Progress," where we will learn about the importance of setting our sights on the future and planning our path to get there.

Section 4: "Infinite Imagination: Unlocking Creative Potential," where we will unlock the boundless potential of our imaginations in shaping our realities.

Each section is a stepping stone on the journey towards a brighter future, guided by the unwavering light of visionary leaders like Dr. Mary McLeod Bethune and Greta Thunberg.

Dreaming and Doing: Envisioning Possibilities

The story of Dr. Bethune begins with a dream. A dream born in the heart of a child who saw education as her pathway to freedom, a dream that grew with her, fueling her determination and resilience, a dream that would eventually transform the lives of countless African Americans. Dr. Bethune dared to dream big, and more importantly, she dared to do, to act on those dreams, to bring them into reality.

Her journey to literacy began with a simple yet profound assertion: "put that down - you can't read." Those words, spoken in defiance of the societal norms of her time, set the stage for the monumental transformation she would catalyze in the coming years. For Dr. Bethune, dreaming and doing were two sides of the same coin. She envisioned a world where her people were not just literate but were also contributors to the rich tapestry of American culture.

Dr. Bethune's words echo with profound wisdom: "Democracy is for me, and for 12 million black Americans, a goal towards which our nation is marching. It is a dream and an ideal in whose ultimate realization we have a deep and abiding faith." She recognized the power of dreaming, of visualizing a brighter future, but she also understood that dreams alone were not enough. Action was necessary to translate those dreams into reality.

In our own lives, we can take inspiration from Dr. Bethune's example. Each of us has dreams, and visions of what we want our future to look like. These dreams act as the North Star, guiding us toward our desired destinations. But like Dr. Bethune, we must be willing to act, to take those necessary steps, however challenging they might be, towards realizing our dreams. Consider Greta Thunberg. As a child, she dreamt of a world where nature was respected and preserved. But she didn't stop at dreaming. She began a solitary protest, striking from school to demand climate action. Her solitary act ignited a global movement, proving that when dreaming is coupled with doing, extraordinary things can happen.

Just as Dr. Bethune's dream led to the establishment of a groundbreaking institution for African-American education, Greta's dream has sparked a global youth movement for climate action. Both women demonstrate the transformative power that lies at the intersection of dreaming and doing. In the same vein, we must not only dare to dream but also dare to do. To translate our dreams into reality, to envision possibilities and bring them into existence, we need to take action. The road might be challenging, and fraught with obstacles and setbacks, but as Dr. Bethune and Greta Thunberg's stories illustrate, the rewards far outweigh the trials.

Hope as a Catalyst: Inspiring Change

The dawn of change begins with the smallest spark, a whisper of a promise that dances on the edges of possibility. It is hope that fuels this spark, hope that transmutes the intangible into the tangible, the possible into reality. Dr. Mary McLeod Bethune was a woman well acquainted with the transformative power of hope.

From the cotton fields of South Carolina to the halls of Washington D.C., hope was Dr. Bethune's constant companion. It was the promise of a better tomorrow that guided her steps and steeled her resolve. As she once stated, "I firmly believe that the world is on its way toward greater unity, that this country is on its way to a fuller realization of democracy, and that the part of the Negro in both movements is one of increased strength and significance." This hope was not a passive desire. It was a catalytic force that drove her to inspire change and challenge the status quo.

The barriers of racial discrimination were high and formidable, but Dr. Bethune refused to be daunted. "All racial barriers, as such, may not fall today or tomorrow but they will not be able to stand long before the determined advance of citizens of all races, shedding their cumbersome, outgrown racial complexes, in the march toward democratic living," she asserted. To Dr. Bethune, hope was not a nebulous concept; it was a tangible force, a motivator that propelled action and instigated change.

We see the echoes of Dr. Bethune's unwavering hope and determination in the actions of contemporary trailblazers. Consider Stacey Abrams, whose tireless fight for voting rights in Georgia embodies the spirit of hope as a catalyst for change.

Despite facing setbacks and opposition, Abrams remained undeterred, her hope in the promise of a more equitable democracy fuelling her perseverance. Her efforts were instrumental in mobilizing voters and flipping Georgia blue in the 2020 presidential elections, a testament to the transformative power of hope.

Much like Dr. Bethune, Stacey Abrams embodies the notion of hope as an active force, not a passive wish. Both women saw hope not just as a dream for a brighter future, but as a call to action. They understood that hoping for change was not enough; one must actively work towards manifesting it. This is a crucial lesson for us all. It teaches us that hope is not merely a comfort in times of despair; it is a tool, a catalyst that can inspire and drive meaningful change.

As we navigate through the trials and tribulations of our lives, we can draw strength from the example set by these remarkable women. We can learn to see hope not just as a beacon in the dark but as a compass guiding us toward our desired destination. We can learn to harness its transformative power, using it to fuel our endeavors and inspire change in our surroundings.

It begins with a shift in perspective, a choice to view hope as an active force rather than a passive wish. It requires us to be proactive, to take the spark of hope and fan it into a flame. It calls for resilience and determination, the courage to keep pushing forward despite the odds.

But most importantly, it requires faith – faith in ourselves, faith in our abilities, and faith in the promise of a brighter tomorrow. As Dr. Bethune so eloquently put it, "We all want the same things. We all intend to get them. We've all been hurt and the hurt affects us in different ways. Hurts are sometimes very useful and serve us better than we sometimes realize. They have drawn us together. They have drawn friends to us. They have made us organization-minded. They have solidified us and our organizations with the organizations of others on an international basis. These hurts have made us united, strong, and determined. We are on our way."

In the same vein, let the hurts, the setbacks, and the disappointments in our lives not be barriers to our progress, but stepping stones. Let them be the catalysts that ignite the spark of hope within us, prompting us to strive harder, reach further, and dream bigger. Let us hold on to the promise of a better tomorrow and let this promise fuel our actions today.

As we step into the next chapter of our lives, let us carry Dr. Bethune's legacy of hope within us. Let us remember her unwavering faith in the promise of a brighter future and her tireless efforts to bring this future into existence. And as we do, let us strive to embody this spirit of hope and determination in our own lives, using it as a catalyst to inspire change and make a difference.

In the following sections, we will delve deeper into the transformative power of hope and explore the ways in which we can harness this power to create meaningful change in our lives. We will look at the importance of dreaming and doing, of envisioning possibilities, and taking concrete steps toward realizing these possibilities. We will also examine the role of planning in progress, discussing the significance of setting clear goals and outlining a roadmap for success. Finally, we will explore the concept of infinite imagination, discussing how we can unlock our creative potential and use it as a tool for transformation.

We invite you to join us on this journey of discovery and transformation, as we explore the lessons from Dr. Mary McLeod Bethune's life and apply them to our own. As we embark on this journey, let us remember that change begins with a single spark, a spark that is fueled by hope and catalyzed by action. And as we journey towards our desired future, let us remember Dr. Bethune's words, "We are on our way."

Future-Focused: Planning for Progress

Dr. Mary McLeod Bethune once said, "Invest in the human soul. Who knows, it might be a diamond in the rough." She understood that the path to a brighter future requires an unwavering focus on growth and progress. Her life was a testament to this belief, as she diligently planned for the advancement of her community and tirelessly worked to turn her vision into reality.

The concept of future-focused planning is not new, but it is more crucial than ever in our rapidly changing world. It is about more than just setting goals; it is about crafting a vision for the future, making strategic decisions, and taking action that aligns with this vision. It requires us to be proactive, not reactive, to anticipate changes, and to adapt accordingly.

Planning for progress begins with setting a clear vision. Dr. Bethune's vision was one of equality, opportunity, and advancement for all. It was a vision that extended beyond her own lifetime, and she dedicated her life to making this vision a reality. She knew that progress is not instantaneous; it is a process that requires time, effort, and patience. Yet, she never wavered from her path, and she remained steadfast in her pursuit of her vision.

Next, planning for progress requires strategic decision-making. This involves assessing our current situation, determining our desired outcome, and identifying the steps necessary to bridge the gap between the two. It involves making tough choices, prioritizing our efforts, and staying focused on our goals, even when faced with obstacles and setbacks. Dr. Bethune exemplified this strategic approach in her work, whether she was establishing a school, advocating for civil rights, or advising presidents.

Finally, planning for progress involves taking consistent action that aligns with our vision and decisions. It's about making our vision tangible through actions and turning our dreams into reality. Dr. Bethune was a woman of action. She didn't just dream of a better future; she rolled up her sleeves and worked to create it. She understood that progress is not handed to us; it is something we must actively pursue.

Planning for progress is not an easy task. It requires courage, resilience, and a relentless commitment to our vision. Yet, as Dr. Bethune's life demonstrates, it is a task that holds immense potential for transformation. In our own lives, we can apply these principles of future-focused planning to our personal and professional goals. Whether we aspire to advance in our careers, improve our health, enrich our relationships, or make a difference in our communities, a clear vision, strategic decisions, and consistent action can guide us toward our desired future.

As we move forward, let us carry Dr. Bethune's spirit of resilience and determination within us. Let us remember her unwavering commitment to progress and her relentless pursuit of her vision. As we do, let us strive to embody these values in our own lives, using them as a guide as we plan for our future and work toward our goals.

Infinite Imagination: Unlocking Creative Potential

Infinite imagination - This was the cornerstone of Dr. Mary McLeod Bethune's life, and she employed it to its full potential. Her success story, one of a child born to former slaves who would go on to be a world-renowned educator, civil rights leader, and advisor to US Presidents, is a testament to the power of imagination. She once said, "The whole world opened to me when I learned to read." This quote exemplifies her belief in the limitless potential of the human mind when it is allowed to imagine, explore, and create. She understood that imagination was not just the ability to form new ideas, but also the catalyst that could bring about significant changes in the world.

Imagination is often associated with creativity and for a good reason. When we allow ourselves to imagine, we break free from the constraints of conventional thinking and open our minds to a world of endless possibilities. This is precisely what Dr. Bethune did. She dared to imagine a world where every child, regardless of their race or background, had access to quality education. This was a radical idea at the time, especially in a society fraught with racial segregation and discrimination. Yet, Dr. Bethune did not let this deter her. Instead, she harnessed her creative potential to transform her imagination into reality, establishing the Bethune-Cookman University, a testament to her visionary leadership.

Dr. Bethune's life teaches us that imagination is not just for the artists, poets, and dreamers of the world. It is a powerful tool that we all possess, one that can inspire us to envision and create a better future for ourselves and others. Unlocking our creative potential requires us to challenge the status quo, to question existing norms and beliefs, and to seek new ways of doing things. It requires us to be open-minded, curious, and willing to take risks. It requires us to believe in the power of our ideas and to have the courage to bring them to life.

As we journey towards our goals, let us embrace the infinite possibilities of our imagination. Let us dare to dream big, to think differently, and to envision a future that exceeds our wildest expectations. And as we do, let us remember Dr. Bethune's legacy of creativity and innovation, and let it inspire us to unlock our creative potential and bring our dreams to life. Embracing the infinite power of imagination is a critical step on our path to personal transformation. It allows us to see beyond our current reality, to envision new possibilities, and to create a future that aligns with our deepest desires and aspirations.

So, my dear reader, I encourage you to unlock your creative potential. Let your imagination soar, and embrace the boundless possibilities that lie before you. And as you do, remember that you carry within you the spirit of Dr. Mary McLeod Bethune, a woman who dared to imagine a better future and had the courage to make it a reality.

Charting Your Course and Taking Action

In the journey through this chapter, we've walked in the footsteps of Dr. Mary McLeod Bethune, a woman who transformed adversity into opportunity, and

whose life was a testament to the power of vision, hope, foresight, and imagination. We've seen how she navigated the challenges of her time, driven by her unwavering faith in the transformative power of education and the boundless potential of the human spirit.

She didn't just dream of a better future, she rolled up her sleeves and made it happen. Through her work, she has shown us that the path to personal transformation begins with envisioning the life we want, fueling it with hope, creating a concrete plan, and unlocking our creative potential to make it a reality. Our journey does not end here, though. It's time now to translate our learning into action. The lessons we've gleaned from Dr. Bethune's life provide us with a blueprint that can guide us on our journey toward achieving our goals. This is the promise that lies before us, an opportunity to seize and make our own.

Now, to help you start, here are five action steps to take:

1. Dream and Envision: Identify your goals and dreams. Don't limit yourself - dare to envision the life you truly desire.
2. Fuel with Hope: Hope is your catalyst. Understand that despite the obstacles you may encounter, you have the power to overcome them.
3. Plan for Progress: Draft a concrete plan for your goal. Break it down into small, manageable steps, and tackle each one at a time.
4. Unlock Your Creative Potential: Allow yourself to think outside the box. Embrace new ideas, and don't be afraid to take unconventional paths towards your goal.
5. Take Action: Start. It doesn't have to be a huge step. Even a small step towards your goal is a step in the right direction.

Dr. Mary McLeod Bethune's life illustrates that transformation is possible when we dare to dream, fuel it with hope, plan for progress, and unleash our creative potential. It is my sincere hope that her life story serves as a guiding light as you embark on your journey towards achieving your goals.

Remember, the future is not something that happens to us - it's something we create. So, go forth and chart your course, dear reader. The world awaits your greatness.

7 Affirmations for this Chapter

1. "In the rich tapestry of history, I am the vibrant thread that ties past heroes to future pioneers; I carry the legacy of Dr. Bethune's visionary optimism."
2. "Every challenge faced by those before me serves as a beacon, illuminating my path towards a brighter and unified future."
3. "I am a part of the powerful movement towards true democracy, where equality, understanding, and respect reign supreme."
4. "The lessons of Dr. Bethune remind me that my journey is not just about personal growth, but also about uplifting and empowering my community."
5. Just as Dr. Bethune saw the potential for greatness in each individual, I too recognize and nurture the brilliance within me and those around me."
6. "I am a testament to the dreams of those who came before me, and I commit to forging a path for those who will come after."
7. "In the face of adversity, I draw strength from the unwavering faith and resilience of icons like Dr. Bethune, knowing that brighter days lie ahead."

These affirmations are rooted in the essence of Dr. Mary McLeod Bethune's teachings, optimism, and commitment to a brighter future for all. They serve to remind and inspire Black women and all readers of their own power and potential in shaping a more inclusive and compassionate world.

With Faith, nothing is Impossible
Bethune Archives-Bethune House Washington, DC

Chapter 10

Mastering Mindfulness: Cultivating Inner Peace

God Is My Source

In the tender hours of a Daytona morning, as the sun draped its warm rays across the Floridian landscape, a woman of stature, imbued with resilience and unyielding spirit, engaged in her morning meditation. Dr. Mary McLeod Bethune, the illustrious educator and activist, shaped history not merely through her tireless activism and educational pursuits, but through a profound commitment to self-care and inner reflection.

Bethune, born of former slaves, was a beacon of hope and a vessel of transformation for the African-American community. Her contributions to education and civil rights are well-known but less recognized is her unwavering commitment to inner well-being, which became evident when she opened the first black hospital in Daytona.

Upon discovering a humble cabin near the school she established, Bethune, through the assistance of generous sponsors, procured the property. In 1911, the Patsy McIntosh McLeod Hospital and Training School for Nurses, named after her mother, was inaugurated. The hospital began as a modest two-bed institution. Still, with Bethune's relentless dedication and the community's trust, it burgeoned to accommodate twenty beds within a few years, serving all races in a time of stark segregation.

Yet, it wasn't only her strides in the physical health sector that resonated; Bethune's spiritual practices held a significant place in her life. As the world around her awakened each morning, she'd sit at her desk in silent meditation, nurturing her spirit before engaging with the day's duties. Her meditations, religious writings, and unwavering faith were not secondary but integral elements of her identity, shaping her approach to education, politics, community, and family.

In the vein of Dr. Bethune's story, a contemporary black woman of influence, Gabrielle Union, openly shares her journey with mental health and self-care. Union's testament of self-reflection and dedication to mental well-being mirrors Bethune's commitment to inner health, bringing these narratives into a modern context.

This chapter promises to guide you through the transformative power of mindfulness and self-care. Drawing inspiration from Bethune's life and Union's experiences, it offers an opportunity to embark on a journey of self-discovery and personal transformation.

In the upcoming sections, we will delve into four inter-twined themes:

1. Conscious Clarity: Embracing Awareness
2. Intentional Introspection: Nurturing Self-Discovery
3. Sacred Stillness: Finding Balance in Chaos
4. Harmonious Healing: Tending to Your Spirit

May you find inspiration, strength, and wisdom within these pages, as you walk your path towards self-discovery and empowerment.

Conscious Clarity: Embracing Awareness

In the labyrinth of life, consciousness serves as a beacon of light, guiding us toward clarity amidst the dense fog of confusion. Dr. Bethune was a shining example of this principle. Her keen awareness of the health disparities in her community was the catalyst for a transformative journey that led to the establishment of the Patsy McIntosh McLeod Hospital.

Bethune's consciousness was not born out of indifference or mere observation of the world around her. It was a deeply ingrained sense of empathy and responsibility towards her people that stirred her into action. Despite the adversities she faced, she maintained an unwavering faith in God, and belief in the power of change, demonstrating that being truly conscious goes beyond merely recognizing a problem. It involves acknowledging the potential for transformation that lies within us and accepting the responsibility to act upon it.

Just as Bethune was conscious of the physical health needs of her community, she was also deeply aware of the importance of mental and spiritual health. Her morning meditations, a testament to her commitment to inner peace and mindfulness, were an integral part of her daily routine. They were her refuge, her source of strength, her moment of clarity amidst the chaos.

Gabrielle Union, like Bethune, has exemplified conscious clarity in her life. By openly sharing her journey with mental health and advocating for self-care, Union has not only highlighted the importance of emotional well-being but has also illuminated the path for others to follow. Her story is a reminder that embracing awareness is the first step toward inner transformation.

As we look closer at the practice of conscious clarity, let us consider its two main components: self-awareness and environmental awareness. Self-awareness involves understanding your emotions, strengths, weaknesses, and beliefs. It is about knowing who you are at your core and embracing your authentic self. Environmental awareness, on the other hand, is about understanding the world around you, the people in it, and the roles you play in your various environments.

For you, the reader, this means embarking on a journey of introspection and observation. It means tuning into your thoughts, emotions, and reactions, and understanding the impact of your environment on your behavior. Embrace this process. Let it unfold naturally. As you do, you will start to see the world, and yourself, with new eyes. In the end, conscious clarity is about understanding that the power to transform your life lies within you. It is about acknowledging that you have the ability to shape your destiny, just as Bethune shaped hers and Union continues to shape hers.

Intentional Introspection: Nurturing Self-Discovery

The journey of self-discovery is a voyage into the depths of your being. It involves peeling back the layers of societal conditioning and self-imposed expectations to reveal your authentic self. This is a path that Dr. Bethune navigated with grace and courage, and it's one that we invite you to embark on. Bethune's introspection was not a fleeting thought or a passing whim; it was intentional, focused, and purposeful. Her morning meditations were not just a practice; they were a sacred ritual that allowed her to connect deeply with herself and her purpose. She was committed to self-discovery, a commitment that fueled her resilience and strengthened her resolve.

Her introspective habits were not confined to her personal life. In her professional sphere, her keen self-awareness and understanding of her community's needs led to the creation of an institution that changed countless lives. This introspection was a driving force behind her transformative impact.

In the modern context, Gabrielle Union's openness about her mental health struggles and her commitment to self-care echo the same spirit of intentional introspection. Union's decision to share her journey was not an easy one. It involved introspecting about her experiences, understanding her mental health needs, and acknowledging the power of vulnerability. This introspection has not only facilitated her healing process but has also inspired many others on their own paths of self-discovery.

For you, the reader, intentional introspection involves taking time to sit with your thoughts, feelings, and experiences, and examining them without judgment. It's about understanding your motivations, your fears, your dreams, and your desires. It's about acknowledging your strengths and weaknesses, your triumphs and failures, and learning from them.

Self-discovery is not a destination; it's an ongoing journey. It's a process of constantly evolving, growing, and transforming. As you engage in intentional introspection, you'll discover aspects of yourself you never knew existed. You'll uncover hidden strengths, buried passions, and a sense of purpose that will guide you on your path to transformation.

Remember, there's no right or wrong way to introspect. The key is to approach it with an open heart and an open mind. Embrace the journey, and let it lead you to the heart of your authentic self.

Sacred Stillness: Finding Balance in Chaos

Amidst the whirlwind of life's trials and tribulations, finding a moment of quietude can seem like an elusive dream. Yet, it is within this sacred stillness that we find our equilibrium, a sense of peace that anchors us even in the face of chaos. For Dr. Bethune, her morning meditations served as her sanctuary of stillness, her oasis of peace amidst the bustling activities of her daily life.

Bethune's life was anything but quiet. She was an educator, a political leader, a civil rights activist, and a hospital founder. Each role came with its own set of challenges and responsibilities, creating a chaotic whirl of duties and demands. Yet, amidst all this, Bethune found her equilibrium in her moments of stillness.

She began her days with meditation, grounding herself in her purpose and aligning her actions with her values. Her moments of stillness were not an escape from the chaos; they were a tool to navigate it. They provided her with the clarity and focus she needed to address the day's challenges and create meaningful change in her community.

Gabrielle Union's journey also resonates with the power of sacred stillness. Her commitment to mental health and self-care, particularly in the face of personal struggles, underscores the importance of finding balance amidst chaos. For Union, self-care routines have been her sanctuary of stillness, her means of maintaining equilibrium in her life.

For you, the reader, finding your sacred stillness means identifying practices that ground you, that bring you peace, and that help you maintain balance amidst the chaos of your life. This could be meditation, as it was for Dr. Bethune, or it could be something else entirely. Perhaps it's a quiet walk in nature, journaling, yoga, or simply sitting in silence for a few minutes each day.

Remember, the goal is not to eliminate chaos - life, by its very nature, is full of challenges and uncertainties. The goal is to find your balance within it, to find your own sacred stillness that helps you navigate life's storms with grace and resilience. Embrace the stillness. Let it permeate your being and bring you back to your center, to your core. Let it be your compass in the chaos, guiding you toward your authentic self and your path to transformation.

Harmonious Healing: Tending to Your Spirit

Healing, in its truest sense, is an all-encompassing journey. It's a gentle process that includes the restoration of balance, the promotion of growth, and the nurturing of the spirit. Dr. Mary McLeod Bethune's life stood as a testament to this journey, showcasing the transformative power of harmonious healing.

Bethune faced challenges that were not only external but also deeply personal and visceral. She was embroiled in societal prejudices, and in her fight for equality and access to education and health facilities, she faced a multitude of hardships. These experiences were powerful and imposing, and they exerted an enormous toll on her spirit. But despite the weight of these adversities, she refused to let bitterness seep into her heart or darken her spirit. Instead, she consciously chose the path of healing.

Bethune's healing was harmonious, and holistic, encompassing not just her physical well-being, but also her mental, emotional, and spiritual health. She tended to her spirit through her unwavering faith, her commitment to morning meditations, and her unyielding dedication to her purpose. Her healing was not merely an isolated incident; it was an ongoing, deeply personal journey that fueled her resilience and amplified her capacity to effect meaningful change.

She understood that healing wasn't just about the physical body, but also about her soul. Healing, to her, was about being whole, about being complete in all aspects of her being. She knew that her spirit needed the same care and attention that her body did. And so, she tended to her spirit, nurturing it with prayer, filling it with love, feeding it with purpose. Gabrielle Union, a contemporary figure whose openness about her mental health journey resonates with many, mirrors the essence of harmonious healing. Union's healing journey involved acknowledging her personal struggles, seeking professional help, and committing to a self-care routine that nurtures her total well-being. This healing process was not linear, nor was it swift; it was a complex journey marked by setbacks, progress, personal growth, and most importantly, self-discovery.

For you, the reader, harmonious healing involves tending to all aspects of your being - physical, mental, emotional, and spiritual. It's about acknowledging your pain, your struggles, and your fears, and choosing to heal from them. It's about nurturing your well-being, fostering self-love, and cultivating resilience. It's about understanding that healing is not just about recovering from a physical ailment. It's about finding peace within yourself, soothing your mind, calming your heart, and nurturing your soul. It's about recognizing that you are a complex, multifaceted being and that all aspects of your being deserve care and attention.

Harmonious healing is a journey of transformation, a journey that leads you closer to your authentic self. As you embark on this healing process, remember that it's okay to seek help, it's okay to experience setbacks, and it's okay to take your time. Healing is not a race; it's a deeply personal journey that unfolds at your own pace. Embrace your healing journey. Let it nurture your spirit, foster your growth, and guide you toward your path of transformation. Remember, every step you take on this journey is a step closer to your authentic self, to the person you are meant to be.

Summary and Action Steps

As we reach the conclusion of this chapter, we reflect on the transformative journey of Dr. Mary McLeod Bethune, a journey marked by consciousness, introspection, balance, and healing. Her life story serves as a beacon, lighting the way toward our own paths of transformation.

Dr. Bethune faced numerous challenges, from societal prejudices to personal hardships. Yet, she did not allow these experiences to embitter her or quench her spirit. Instead, she chose to rise above, choosing to heal, choosing transformation. Her life was a testament to the power of resilience, the power of faith, and the power of purpose. Likewise, Gabrielle Union's openness about her mental health journey mirrors the essence of this transformative path. Her journey speaks of courage, of self-discovery, and of resilience, reminding us that healing and transformation are possible, regardless of our circumstances.

For you, the reader, this chapter serves as an invitation to embark on your own transformative journey. It calls you to embrace consciousness, to nurture introspection, to find balance in chaos, and to tend to your spirit. It invites you to uncover your authentic self, to step into your power, and to live your purpose. As you move forward, remember that transformation is a journey, not a destination. It unfolds at your own pace, in your own time. Embrace each step, each moment, and each experience, for they are all part of your unique path toward transformation.

Here are five action steps to guide you on your journey:

1. Cultivate Consciousness: Begin your day with a moment of silence. Use this time to tune into your thoughts, your feelings, and your inner world. Cultivate an awareness of yourself, your experiences, and your environment.
2. Nurture Introspection: Set aside time each day for self-reflection. Ask yourself questions like, 'What am I feeling?' 'What do I need?' 'What is my purpose?' Use these moments of introspection to deepen your understanding of yourself and your journey.
3. Find Balance: Practice mindfulness in your daily life. Whether you're working, spending time with loved ones, or simply enjoying a moment of solitude, strive to be fully present. Find balance amidst the chaos of life.
4. Tend to Your Spirit: Engage in activities that nourish your spirit. This could be anything from prayer, meditation, spending time in nature, or engaging in creative pursuits. Listen to what your spirit needs and honor those needs.
5. Commit to Healing: Acknowledge your pain, your struggles, and your fears, and choose to heal from them. Seek help if needed, and remember that it's okay to take your time. Healing is a journey, one that you navigate at your own pace.

In conclusion, remember that you, just like Dr. Mary McLeod Bethune and Gabrielle Union, have the power to transform your life. Embrace your journey, nurture your spirit, and step into your greatness. Your transformation awaits.

7 Affirmations for Chapter 10: Mastering Mindfulness: Cultivating Inner Peace

1. "I channel the resilience of Dr. Bethune, finding clarity and purpose in each moment."

2. "In the stillness of my heart, I connect with my ancestors, drawing strength and wisdom from their journey."
3. "Each day, I honor the sacredness of my being, embracing awareness and growth with every breath."
4. "Like Dr. Bethune, I see challenges as doorways to introspection and transformation, guiding me closer to my true self."
5. "In the midst of chaos, I find my sacred stillness, grounding myself in the love and legacy of those who came before me."
6. "I nurture my spirit with the teachings of trailblazers, allowing their stories to illuminate my path to harmonious healing."
7. "Embracing my history, I step forward with intention and grace, realizing the transformative power of mindfulness in my life."

These affirmations, inspired by Dr. Mary McLeod Bethune's legacy and the essence of Chapter 10, serve as daily reminders of the power of introspection, awareness, and connection to one's roots. They aim to fortify the reader's journey to inner peace and purpose.

In My Solitude
Bethune House - Archive

Chapter 11

Bountiful Blessings: Cultivating Gratitude and Generosity

There is Great Strength in Gratitude

As we embark on this chapter, we turn our focus to a paramount virtue that Dr. Mary McLeod Bethune embodied throughout her life - generosity. Beyond her educational endeavors and political activism, Dr. Bethune had a heart that spilled over with kindness and philanthropy. She viewed these virtues as blessings and gifts to be shared with the world. Dr. Bethune's life was a living testament to the philosophy that giving and receiving are two sides of the same coin. She understood that gratitude was the key to recognizing abundance, and generosity was the mechanism through which that abundance could circulate and grow.

Her acts of kindness and philanthropy were plentiful and varied. She led war bond drives, and blood donation drives, and encouraged African-American women to staff the canteens that dotted the country. In 1931, her remarkable efforts were recognized nationally when she was listed tenth on a list of the most outstanding living American women. She used her platform to push an agenda for racial and gender inclusion and championed conventional family life for racial uplift.

Dr. Bethune was introduced to the Roosevelts in 1927 and later supported their run for the Presidency. The close friendship with Eleanor Roosevelt was instrumental in gaining regular access to the President. In 1936, President Roosevelt tasked her to join the National Youth Administration and by 1939 she became the Director of Negro Affairs. As Director, Bethune was the highest-paid African-American in government at the time —with a $5,000 salary. Under her guidance as Director, NYA employed hundreds of thousands of young African-American men and women and established a "Negro College and Graduate Fund" that supported over 4,000 students in higher education.

Her philanthropy was not limited to the realm of education. She led many community drives to register voters and faced the wrath of the KKK. Even amid danger, she never wavered from her mission to uplift and empower her community. Her legacy of generosity and community service carried on until her passing on May 18, 1955.

Historian Audrey Thomas McCluskey summed it up best when she wrote: "Despite the numerous instances of racism shown toward her, and even unsubstantiated charges that she was a Communist sympathizer, Bethune maintained her belief in America." She possessed unwavering patriotism, a strong sense of racial pride, and even walked with a cane that had once belonged to her friend, President Franklin Roosevelt.

Reflecting on Dr. Bethune's life, one can't help but draw parallels to the modern-day philanthropic endeavors of influential women, such as the globally recognized pop icon, Rihanna. Through the Clara Lionel Foundation, Rihanna has been making significant strides in areas of education and emergency response programs. Like Dr. Bethune, Rihanna uses her platform to promote social change and uplift communities, embodying the spirit of generosity in her actions.

Let us proceed to the next section where we delve into the concept of gratitude as a gift and explore the idea of embracing abundance in our lives.

Gratitude as a Gift: Embracing Abundance

Gratitude is a potent and transformative force. It is a beacon of light that illuminates our lives, even in the darkest of times. It is the ability to look beyond what is lacking, to see and appreciate the abundance that life has to offer. It was this mindset of gratitude that equipped Dr. Mary McLeod Bethune with the resilience to rise above the circumstances of her birth and forge a path of greatness.

Born to former slaves, Dr. Bethune was no stranger to hardship. Yet, she chose to focus not on the hardship, but on the opportunities that were before her. She reveled in the gift of literacy, a gift she fervently believed should be shared. Through her tireless efforts, she founded the Daytona Educational and Industrial School for Negro Girls, a testament to her commitment to sharing her gift of education.

Dr. Bethune's life was an embodiment of gratitude in action. It was a gratitude that was not complacent, but rather dynamic and compelling. Her appreciation for her blessings ignited in her an unwavering desire to give back, to lift others as she climbed.

As we journey through our lives, let us strive to embody this same spirit of gratitude. Let us learn to recognize the abundance that surrounds us. Each day, we are blessed with countless gifts - the warmth of the sun, the support of loved ones, the opportunity to learn and grow. These are blessings that are too often overlooked.

Begin by cultivating a daily practice of gratitude. Perhaps you could keep a gratitude journal, where each day, you record three things for which you are thankful. This practice forces us to shift our focus from scarcity to abundance, enabling us to recognize the wealth of blessings that we often take for granted.

Gratitude is more than mere words of thanks. It is a deep, heartfelt appreciation that can radically shift our perception of the world. It encourages us to move from a mindset of lack to one of abundance. It is the first step in fostering a spirit of generosity, a trait that was deeply engrained in Dr. Bethune's character and one that we will explore in the next section.

Generous Giving: Sharing Your Wealth and Wisdom

As we journey through the transformative narrative of Dr. Mary McLeod Bethune, the concept of generous giving emerges as a cornerstone of her legacy. Yet, in discussing generosity, it is essential to clarify that the wealth Dr. Bethune shared wasn't simply materialistic or financial; it was an all-encompassing outpouring of knowledge, time, wisdom, and unwavering commitment to serving others. Her life provides us with a richer, more nuanced understanding of what it means to give and the profound impact that such giving can have on our lives and the lives of those around us.

Born into a family of former slaves, Dr. Bethune could have let her circumstances dictate her path. Instead, she chose to rise above them and transform them into a catalyst for change. Her journey wasn't easy; it was fraught with challenges and obstacles. Yet, she remained undeterred, buoyed by an un-shakeable belief in the transformative power of education and the potential for greatness within each individual.

Her determination led her to establish the Daytona Educa-tional and Industrial Training School for Negro Girls, an insti-tution that would later become Bethune-Cookman University. This remarkable feat was a testament to Dr. Bethune's phi-losophy of generous giving. She understood that sharing the wealth of knowledge she had acquired was the most significant gift she could offer her community.

Her school was more than just a place of learning; it was a beacon of hope in a society riddled with racial prejudice and in-equality. It represented the promise of a better future, a future where African Americans had the right to education, dignity, and the pursuit of their dreams. In creating this institution, Dr. Bethune didn't just share her wealth; she invested it in the lives of her students, fostering a culture of empowerment that continues to thrive today.

Generous giving, as Dr. Bethune demonstrated, isn't a one-time act; it's a lifelong commitment. Throughout her life, she continued to give her time and energy to causes that up-lifted African Americans. From leading war bond drives to championing civil rights, she used her influence and resources to drive change. Her example serves as a powerful reminder that each one of us has a wealth of gifts to offer. These gifts may not be monetary, but they hold immense value. Perhaps you possess a talent for music, a knack for problem-solving, or a comforting presence that brings solace to those in distress. Recognize these gifts and embrace the opportunities to share them.

Consider how you might contribute to your community. Can you offer mentorship to a young person in need of guidance? Could you volunteer your time at a local organization? Could you use your skills to support a cause that resonates with you? Remember, the act of giving should be a joy, not a burden. It's not about what you stand to gain but what you can help others achieve.

That said, it's also important to maintain a balance. Generosity should never come at the cost of your own well-being. True giving is sustainable, enriching not just the receiver but also the giver. As we adopt a spirit of generous giving, we find that our lives become richer, our connections stronger, and our sense of purpose more profound. In the next section, we'll delve deeper into these connections, exploring the role of compassion in forging meaningful relationships and fostering a sense of unity.

Compassionate Connection: Fostering Empathy

The narrative of Dr. Mary McLeod Bethune's life is a testament to the power of compassion in forging deep and meaningful connections. She believed that empathy was the foundation of a just and inclusive society, and she strived to foster it within her community and beyond. The empathy Dr.

Bethune embodied wasn't merely a passive form of understanding; it was an active engagement with the struggles and experiences of others. It propelled her to advocate for those in need, to be a voice for the voiceless, and to work tirelessly to improve the lives of those around her. This active empathy was apparent in her many roles - an educator, a civil rights activist, a government official, and a philanthropist.

Consider her work with the National Youth Administration (NYA). When President Roosevelt appointed her as the Director of Negro Affairs, Dr. Bethune saw an opportunity to make a tangible difference in the lives of young African Americans. Under her leadership, the NYA provided employment and education opportunities for hundreds of thousands of African-American youths. She recognized the potential in these young individuals and worked to ensure they had the resources and support to realize their dreams. This was empathy in action.

Dr. Bethune's compassionate connection also extended to her prison ministry. Even while juggling her responsibilities as an educator and activist, she made time to visit prisoners, offering solace and hope to those often forgotten by society. She saw beyond their circumstances and recognized their inherent worth and dignity.

In forging these connections, Dr. Bethune demonstrated the transformative power of empathy. But how can we cultivate such empathy within ourselves? Here are a few strategies:

- Active Listening: Truly hearing someone's story is the first step towards understanding their experiences. Practice active listening by giving your undivided attention to

the person speaking, showing genuine interest, and ask-
ing open-ended questions to encourage deeper sharing.
- **Perspective-Taking:** Try to put yourself in the other
person's shoes. Imagining their thoughts, feelings, and
experiences can help you understand their perspective
better.
- **Common Humanity:** Remember that we're all part of the
human family, with shared emotions, needs, and desires.
Recognizing our common humanity can foster empathy
and dissolve barriers of 'us' and 'them'.
- **Mindful Awareness:** Being present in the moment allows
us to be more attuned to the emotions and experiences of
others. Practicing mindfulness can enhance our capacity
for empathy.

By fostering empathetic connections, we create a ripple
effect of kindness and understanding in our communities. We
build bridges instead of walls and promote a culture of inclusivity and respect. And just as Dr. Bethune's compassionate
connections left a lasting legacy, so can ours.

In the next section, we'll explore the concept of purposeful
philanthropy, a natural progression from empathy and compassionate connection. We'll look at how Dr. Bethune's life
provides valuable lessons in using our resources, talents, and
time to make a positive impact on our community and the
world.

Purposeful Philanthropy: Leaving a Lasting Impact

Dr. Mary McLeod Bethune's life was a symphony of purposeful philanthropy, underscored by her undying belief in the
power of education and her commitment to the upliftment of
the Black community. Her actions exemplify what it means to

devote oneself to a cause greater than oneself, leaving a lasting impact that echoes through generations.

Take a moment to envision the Daytona Educational and Industrial School for Negro Girls, a small school that Dr. Bethune established in 1904 with a mere $1.50 to her name. She started with only six pupils, but she had a vision — a vision of creating a beacon of hope and opportunity for Black girls in a deeply segregated society.

With unwavering determination, Dr. Bethune transformed this vision into a reality. She solicited donations, sold sweet potato pies, and even made use of discarded railway station benches for her school. Her drive to procure funds and resources was relentless because she believed in the transformative power of education.

Over time, her small school blossomed into what is now known as Bethune-Cookman University, a fully accredited institution that has produced generations of successful graduates. Dr. Bethune's purposeful philanthropy laid the foundation for a legacy that continues to uplift countless lives today.

And yet, Dr. Bethune's philanthropic efforts went beyond the realm of education. She leveraged her influence to advocate for civil rights and women's rights, tirelessly campaigning for equality and justice. She served as a special assistant to the Secretary of War for the Women's Army Auxiliary Corps, ensuring that Black women had access to army officer training. Through her work with the National Youth Administration, she secured employment and higher education opportunities for hundreds of thousands of young African Americans.

These actions, and many others, were a testament to Dr. Bethune's approach to philanthropy — an approach that was deeply purposeful, passionately committed, and broadly encompassing. So, what can we glean from Dr. Bethune's life of purposeful philanthropy?

First, philanthropy goes beyond monetary donations. It involves giving your time, your skills, your voice, and your influence to effect positive change. Whether it's mentoring a young person, advocating for a cause, or volunteering at a local charity, there are countless ways to make a difference.

Second, purposeful philanthropy is driven by a deep commitment to a cause that resonates with your core values. For Dr. Bethune, this cause was the empowerment of the Black community through education and civil rights. What cause resonates with your heart? What can you do to support that cause?

Finally, remember that every effort counts, no matter how small. Dr. Bethune started with a single schoolroom and a handful of students, but she changed the world. Never underestimate the power of purposeful action.

As we prepare to conclude this chapter, let's carry forward the lessons gleaned from Dr. Bethune's life. Embrace gratitude, share generously, foster empathy, and pursue purposeful philanthropy. In doing so, we honor her legacy and continue the work she began.

Action Steps

Dr. Mary McLeod Bethune's life was a testament to the power of gratitude, generosity, empathy, and purposeful philanthropy. Her story is a beacon that shines brightly, guiding us toward a life of purpose and fulfillment. It is a reminder that we, too, possess the capacity to cultivate these virtues within ourselves and wield them as tools for transformation.

Dr. Bethune transformed the adversity she faced into fuel for change, never losing sight of her vision for a brighter future for her community. She cultivated a deep sense of gratitude, understanding that every experience, every challenge, and every triumph was a stepping stone on her journey. She shared generously, giving not only her resources but also her wisdom, her time, and her heart. Dr. Bethune fostered empathy, always striving to understand and uplift those around her. Finally, she embarked on a path of purposeful philanthropy, leaving a lasting impact that continues to inspire us today.

Now, it is time for us to apply these lessons to our lives. It is time for us to step into our power and embody the spirit of Dr. Bethune. Here are five action steps to guide you on this journey:

Action Step 1:
Cultivate Gratitude - Start a gratitude journal. Each day, write down three things you are grateful for. They could be as simple as a sunny day or a kind word from a friend. This practice will help you develop an attitude of gratitude.

Action Step 2:
Practice Generosity - Find a way to give back to your community. This could involve donating to a local charity, volunteering your time, or sharing your skills with those in need.

Action Step 3:
Foster Empathy - Seek to understand the experiences and perspectives of others. This could involve having meaningful conversations with people who come from different back-

grounds or reading books that broaden your understanding of diverse experiences.

Action Step 4:

Engage in Purposeful Philanthropy - Identify a cause that resonates deeply with you and find a way to support it. This could involve fundraising, advocacy, or volunteering.

Action Step 5:

Reflect on Your Impact - Take time to reflect on the difference you are making in your community. How have your actions positively impacted others? Use these reflections to fuel your continued journey of transformation.

As you embark on this journey, remember the words of Dr. Bethune: "The whole world opened to me when I learned to read." The world opens to us when we read and learn from the stories of trailblazers like Dr. Bethune. By cultivating gratitude, practicing generosity, fostering empathy, and engaging in purposeful philanthropy, we honor her legacy and open the door to our own transformation.

7 Affirmations for this Chapter

1. "I am inspired by the strength of trailblazers like Dr. Bethune and channel that energy into my own path of purpose."
2. "Every act of kindness I give ripples out into the world, creating a legacy of love and compassion."
3. "I embrace gratitude daily, recognizing the abundance surrounding me and the powerful ancestors guiding me."
4. "Generosity is a reflection of my inner wealth, and I generously share my wisdom and resources to uplift my community."

5. "Empathy is my bridge to deeper connections, under-standing, and unity with those around me."
6. "Like Dr. Bethune, I am creating a lasting impact, leaving footsteps for future generations to find their way."
7. "I am on a transformative journey, drawing strength from the stories of Black icons, and I honor that legacy in every step I take."

BE BETHUNE
Dr, Mary McLeod Bethune Foundation, Inc.

Chapter 12

Legacy of Love: Embodying the Spirit of Dr. Mary McLeod Bethune

In the annals of Black history, a woman's name echoes with resilience and determination: Dr. Mary McLeod Bethune. Dr. Bethune was a woman who transformed the lives of many, and whose legacy continues to empower us today. Born to parents who had known the shackles of slavery, she grew up in a world of adversity and discrimination. Yet, she dared to dream. She dared to believe. And, with that belief, she dared to transform.

There was a time, in the early years of her school, when it was on the brink of closure due to lack of funds. The problem was dire, and the solution seemed out of reach. How could she keep the doors open? How could she continue to offer the beacon of education to the young Black children who so desperately needed it?

In her darkest hour, Dr. Bethune did something extraordinary. She baked sweet potato pies. Yes, you read that right. Dr. Bethune, in her moment of crisis, turned to her roots. She baked sweet potato pies and sold them to the workers at the local dump. The sweet aroma of her pies drew the workers in, and the delicious taste kept them coming back for more. The funds she raised through her humble pies were enough to keep the school afloat. Her determination turned a problem into a solution, and from there, her school grew, expanding its influence and reach. It would later become Bethune-Cookman University, a monument to her indomitable spirit.

Today, we see echoes of Dr. Bethune's spirit in women like Beyoncé. Through her philanthropy and artistic contributions, Beyoncé uplifts the Black community, using her platform to shine a spotlight on issues that matter. Like Dr. Bethune, she turns challenges into opportunities, creating spaces where Black excellence can thrive. The promise that emerges from their stories is profound: that you, too, can transform obstacles into opportunities. You, too, can leave a legacy that resonates through the ages.

In this chapter, we will delve into the timeless teachings of Dr. Bethune, examining how her life of service can inspire and guide us today. We will explore how to honor her legacy and follow in her footsteps, ultimately embracing our destiny and purpose. The journey to greatness is a journey inward. It is a journey of self-discovery, of realizing our potential, and of harnessing our power. Join us as we embark on this journey, guided by the lessons of Dr. Mary McLeod Bethune.

Timeless Teachings: Applying Dr. Bethune's Lessons - Extended Version

In the grand tapestry of history, we often find transformative figures who rise above their circumstances to change the world. Dr. Mary McLeod Bethune was one such extraordinary woman. Born on a small farm in South Carolina in 1875, she was the fifteenth child of 17 children of former slaves. Her early life, filled with hardship and poverty, was reflective of the struggles that the Black community in America faced during that time. Yet, she dared to dream. In the face of adversity, she saw not barriers, but opportunities. Opportunities to learn, to grow, and to transform.

Her parents, Samuel and Patsy McIntosh McLeod, valued education and its potential to lift them out of poverty, even though they themselves were illiterate. The seeds of their belief were planted in their daughter Mary. It was this unflinching belief in the power of education that would guide her future actions and form the bedrock of her legacy.

Dr. Bethune believed in the transformative power of education. She was the only one in her family who had the opportunity to attend school, a privilege she did not take lightly. She knew that knowledge could break the chains of ignorance and prejudice. It could empower individuals and uplift communities. It was this understanding that guided her as she founded the Daytona Normal and Industrial Institute for Negro Girls in 1904, a school that would later become the Bethune-Cookman University. It was a monumental task, one that she undertook with a singular determination and a vision for a future where every Black child had access to quality education.

Through her journey, she faced numerous challenges. There were times when the school had no funding, and she had to do odd jobs to keep it running. She faced the scorn of those who did not believe in her vision. Yet, she never gave up. Instead, she found innovative ways to overcome these challenges. She baked sweet potato pies and fried fish, selling them to workers at nearby construction sites to raise funds for her school. She faced every challenge head-on, with an unwavering resolve and a deep faith in her mission. Her story reminds us that it is not the size of the obstacle that matters, but the strength of our determination to overcome it.

In the digital age, we live in a world where information is at our fingertips. Yet, the value of education remains unchanged. It is the key to understanding our world, our history, and ourselves. As Dr. Bethune once said, "Knowledge is the prime need of the hour." Dr. Bethune's life also embodied the power of community. She understood that the struggle for equality was not a solitary battle but a collective effort. She rallied her community, inspiring them with her vision and her unwavering belief in their potential. She knew that to uplift one was to uplift all.

In our lives, we can apply this lesson by recognizing the strength of our community. By supporting each other, we can collectively overcome challenges and achieve our goals. We can create a ripple effect of positivity and progress that can transform not only our lives but also the lives of those around us. Another timeless teaching from Dr. Bethune's life is the power of purpose. She found her purpose in empowering others through education. This purpose guided her actions and gave her the strength to persevere in the face of adversity.

Finding our purpose can be a transformative journey. It can give our lives direction and meaning. It can inspire us to pursue our dreams and make a difference in the world. Dr. Bethune's life serves as a reminder that, with purpose, we can overcome any obstacle and achieve greatness.

Dr. Mary McLeod Bethune's legacy is a testament to the power of education, community, and purpose. Her life is a blueprint for us to follow as we navigate our own journeys. As modern women, we can draw inspiration from her strength and resilience. We can learn from her unwavering belief in the power of education and her commitment to her community. We can find strength in her purpose and her unyielding determination to make a difference. Her life serves as a beacon of hope, guiding us toward our own paths of self-discovery and empowerment.

Looking at our contemporary society, we find echoes of Dr. Bethune's life in the actions of many influential Black women. Take, for instance, the internationally acclaimed artist and philanthropist, Beyoncé Knowles-Carter. In addition to her significant contributions to the world of music and entertainment, Beyoncé has made a profound impact on her community through her philanthropic efforts.

In 2018, Beyoncé and her husband, Jay-Z, announced a new scholarship program called The BeyGOOD Initiative and the Shawn Carter Foundation. The program aims to "help eliminate the barriers to higher education" and provide scholarships to students in need. This effort echoes Dr. Bethune's commitment to education and her belief in its transformative power. Beyoncé, much like Dr. Bethune, recognizes the value of education and is using her platform to provide opportunities for the next generation.

In this chapter, we will delve deeper into the timeless teachings of Dr. Mary McLeod Bethune. We will explore how her life's lessons can be applied in our own lives, and how we can draw strength from her example. We will discuss the enduring impact of her life and her legacy, and how we can honor her by living a life of service. We will also explore how we can follow in her footsteps, embracing our destiny and purpose, and soaring to greatness.

Are you ready to embark on this journey with me? Are you ready to dive deeper into the life of this remarkable woman and uncover the lessons she has left behind for us? If so, let us begin. Section 2 will take a deeper look into the lessons from Dr. Bethune's life and how we can apply them in our own lives. We'll explore her teachings on education, community, and purpose, and how they can serve as a guide for us in our journeys of self-discovery and empowerment.

In Section 3, we'll discuss the enduring impact of Dr. Bethune's life and how we can honor her legacy by living a life of service. We'll delve into her vision of upliftment through collective action and the lessons we can learn from her dedication to her community.

In Section 4, we'll delve into how we can follow in Dr. Bethune's footsteps, embracing our destiny and purpose, and soaring to greatness. We'll explore the power of purpose and how it can guide us in our journey toward self-fulfillment and empowerment.

Eternal Echoes: Honoring a Life of Service

In honoring the legacy of Dr. Mary McLeod Bethune, one cannot neglect her tireless efforts on the international stage. Dr. Bethune, as a visionary leader, was deeply conscious of the universality of human struggles and the interconnectedness of the human experience. She understood that the fight for equality and justice was not confined to the borders of her homeland but was a global endeavor. Her vision extended far beyond the walls of her classrooms, reaching out to touch the lives of people in distant corners of the world.

Dr. Bethune's involvement with the Moral Re-Armament (MRA) was an expression of her commitment to peace, unity, and moral integrity. The MRA, a global movement initiated in the 1930s, aimed to build a world of peace and justice by transforming individuals' attitudes and behaviors. Dr. Bethune saw in the MRA a moral compass, a guide to nurture the essential virtues of honesty, purity, unselfishness, and love. By working with MRA, she reinforced her belief in the capacity of moral and spiritual transformation to bring about social change.

Her relationship with W.E.B. Du Bois, a fellow pioneer in the fight for racial equality, offered her the intellectual stimulation and emotional support that fueled her endeavors. They shared a mutual respect and admiration that transcended their professional association. Their correspondence, which spanned over three decades, revealed a bond of friendship rooted in shared experiences and a collective vision for a racially inclusive society. Du Bois' influence on Dr. Bethune's work was profound, shaping her understanding of race, class, and the struggle for human rights.

Dr. Bethune's love for art and culture found resonance in the Harlem Renaissance, an explosion of African-American cultural expression in the 1920s and 1930s. She was deeply influenced by the works of Langston Hughes, Zora Neale Hurston, and other creative minds of the time. These artists used their craft to challenge racial prejudice and celebrate Black identity, a theme that resonated deeply with Dr. Bethune. She believed that the arts could serve as powerful tools for social change, inspiring individuals to challenge the status quo and envision a more inclusive society.

Her commitment to racial equality was not limited to the realm of education. Dr. Bethune was deeply involved in advocating for the integration of the armed services and the inclusion of Black nurses in the military. She understood that segregation in any form was an affront to the ideals of justice and equality. Through her advocacy, she helped pave the way for greater representation and recognition of Black contributions in the military, reinforcing her belief in the potential of each individual to make a difference.

Through her international work, moral advocacy, intellectual collaborations, and love for arts and culture, Dr. Bethune worked tirelessly to move America away from its racist history. Her life serves as a testament to the power of determination, resilience, and moral conviction in effecting social change. As we delve deeper into her legacy, let's draw inspiration from her unwavering commitment to service and her enduring belief in the transformative power of education.

Next, we will explore how we can follow in her footsteps, embody her teachings, and draw strength from her legacy to achieve greatness in our own lives. We will discover how to channel her spirit of resilience and determination, her commitment to service, and her unyielding faith in the power of education to transform lives and societies.

Emboldened by Example: Following in Her Footsteps

As we walk the path that Dr. Mary McLeod Bethune has paved, we are not simply retracing her steps but forging our own unique path using the lessons she left us. Each stride taken is a testament to her resilience, each victory an homage to her indomitable spirit, and every challenge we overcome a tribute to her unwavering determination.

Dr. Bethune's life was one of relentless pursuit and tireless dedication to her cause. Her courage, her conviction, and her unwavering faith in her mission should serve as an inspirational beacon for every woman seeking to make a difference in her world. Her relationship with giants of the time like W.E.B. Du Bois, Langston Hughes, and Zora Neale Hurston informs us of her intellectual curiosity and her desire to be part of the broader cultural and intellectual discourse of her era. She embraced their work and their struggles, giving them a platform at Bethune-Cookman College, where she included art, music, and literature as integral components of the curriculum.

Just like Dr. Bethune, you too can harness the power of relationships and collaboration to further your mission. Embrace intellectual discourse, seek knowledge and different perspectives, and never be afraid to challenge the status quo. Surround yourself with people who uplift you, challenge you, and inspire you to strive for greatness.

Dr. Bethune's involvement with the Moral Re-Armament, (MRA) movement teaches us the importance of grounding our actions in a solid moral foundation. It is not enough to merely aspire to greatness; we must be guided by principles of honesty, integrity, and a deep-seated commitment to justice. As you traverse your path to greatness, let these principles guide you. They are the compass that will steer you towards meaningful success.

Taking a cue from Dr. Bethune's advocacy for racial equality in the military, we learn the power of taking a stand, of fighting for what we believe in, regardless of the odds stacked against us. In the face of systemic racism and deep-seated prejudice, she fought for the inclusion of Black nurses in the military, a feat that seemed impossible at the time. Yet, she persevered, and her efforts bore fruit.

Just as she did, you can make a difference in your world, whether it's advocating for equality in your workplace, campaigning for social justice in your community, or lending your voice to causes that matter to you. No action is too small, no effort is insignificant.

Lastly, remember that Dr. Bethune's journey was not devoid of hardships and struggles. Yet, she remained resilient, drawing strength from her faith and her unyielding belief in her mission. Her resilience is a beacon for every woman navigating the tumultuous seas of life. When faced with adversity, remember her words: "We have a powerful potential in our youth, and we must have the courage to change old ideas and practices so that we may direct their power toward good ends."

In the next section, we will explore how to harness the lessons from Dr. Bethune's life to soar to greatness and achieve our destiny and purpose. Remember, your journey is your own, but you're not alone; you walk in the footsteps of a woman who blazed a trail for us all.

Soaring to Greatness: Embracing Your Destiny and Purpose

Dr. Mary McLeod Bethune once said, "I leave you love. I leave you hope. I leave you the challenge of developing confidence in one another. I leave you a thirst for education. I leave you respect for the use of power. I leave you faith. I leave you racial dignity."

These powerful words encapsulate the essence of her journey and the legacy she left for us to build upon. To soar to greatness, you must first embrace your destiny and purpose with the same fervor and dedication that Dr. Bethune demonstrated in her lifetime.

You may wonder, how do we unearth our purpose, our destiny? It starts with introspection and self-awareness, knowing who you are and what you truly value. Dr. Bethune was a woman deeply grounded in her identity, her faith, and her love for her people. She knew her purpose was to uplift the African-American community through education and social activism, and she dedicated her life to this cause.

Like Dr. Bethune, you must recognize that your purpose is bigger than you. It is a cause that resonates with your soul, something you are deeply passionate about. It could be anything, from fighting for social justice and advocating for educational equity to empowering women. Once you uncover your purpose, dedicate yourself to it wholeheartedly, as Dr. Bethune did.

Your destiny, on the other hand, is the unique path you carve in the pursuit of your purpose. It is the journey you embark upon to make your mark in the world. Dr. Bethune's destiny led her from the cotton fields of South Carolina to the corridors of power in Washington, D.C., shaping the course of American history along the way.

To embrace your destiny, you must be willing to step out of your comfort zone and take risks. Dr. Bethune risked everything to establish Bethune-Cookman College. She took on the burden of debt, faced skepticism and criticism, and yet persevered because she knew this was her destiny. Don't be afraid of the challenges and obstacles that will inevitably come your way. They are but stepping stones on your path to greatness.

As we soar to greatness, let us remember to do so with love, hope, and faith, as Dr. Bethune taught us. Love for ourselves, for each other, and for our communities. Hope for a better future and the confidence to bring about the change we wish to see. Faith in our abilities, in our purpose, and in our destiny. In the final section, we'll summarize the chapter, and offer actionable steps to embody the spirit of Dr. Mary McLeod Bethune, to help you navigate your journey to greatness. So, as you embrace your destiny and purpose, remember, in the words of Dr. Bethune, "The whole world opened to me when I learned to read."

Embodying the Spirit of Dr. Mary McLeod Bethune

The Life of Dr. Mary McLeod Bethune teaches valuable lessons she left behind. A remarkable woman who overcame adversity and left an indelible mark on the world, her story is a testament to the power of resilience, courage, and purposeful living. Through her life, we've seen how it is possible to transcend our circumstances, achieve greatness, and effect meaningful change, irrespective of our backgrounds or the hurdles we confront.

Dr. Bethune's life was a shining beacon that illuminated the path of progress, not just for African Americans, but for all marginalized communities. She demonstrated that with unwavering determination, commitment, and a strong belief in God, there's no limit to what we can achieve. In learning about her journey, we come to understand the critical role we each play in shaping our society and the immense potential we each carry to make a difference in our world.

Now, let's outline actionable steps inspired by Dr. Bethune's life that can guide us in our own journey of transformation:

- **Commit to lifelong learning:** Dr. Bethune's life demonstrated a fervent belief in the transformative power of education. She once said, "Knowledge is the prime need of the hour." Embrace this ethos by investing in your personal growth and intellectual development. This could be through formal education, self-study, webinars, workshops, or merely engaging in enriching conversations. Lifelong learning is a journey, not a destination. Remember, every day presents a new opportunity to learn something new.
- **Connect with your community:** Dr. Bethune was deeply engaged with her community. She worked tirelessly not just for her personal success but the upliftment of those around her. Identify ways you can contribute to your community, whether that's through volunteering, mentoring, or participating in local initiatives. As you rise, lift others with you – that's the essence of community.
- **Foster supportive relationships:** Sisterhood and collaboration were central themes in Dr. Bethune's life. The relationships she forged with other Black intellectuals and activists of her time, such as W.E.B. Du Bois, Langston Hughes, and Zora Neale Hurston, significantly shaped her work and influence. Surround yourself with individuals who motivate you, share your values, and push you to achieve your goals. Together, you can overcome obstacles and celebrate milestones.
- **Cultivate resilience:** Dr. Bethune's journey was fraught with adversity, yet she never gave up. She faced each

challenge with courage and emerged stronger. Adopt a similar mindset. View setbacks as stepping stones to growth and let them strengthen your resolve.

· **Live purposefully:** Dr. Bethune devoted her life to a cause greater than herself – the upliftment of African Americans through education and social activism. Discover your unique purpose and channel your energies toward fulfilling it. Doing so not only leads to personal satisfaction but contributes to a better world.

In essence, Dr. Mary McLeod Bethune's life and legacy provide us with a roadmap to personal transformation and societal impact. Her story is a clarion call to action, urging us to step into our power, live our truth, and contribute to the collective good. As we journey towards realizing our full potential, let's keep Dr. Bethune's spirit alive within us.

Remember, as Dr. Bethune once said, "Invest in the human soul. Who knows, it might be a diamond in the rough." Let us heed these words and strive to become the best versions of ourselves, honoring Dr. Bethune's legacy and carrying her spirit forward. Our journey to greatness has only just begun. Are you ready to embrace your destiny and follow in the footsteps of this remarkable woman? As Dr. Bethune did, let's rise above our circumstances, uplift those around us, and create a legacy that future generations will honor and cherish.

Dr. Mary McLeod Bethune's story is a testament to the indomitable spirit of human resilience and the transformative power of purpose. As we incorporate her teachings into our lives, we too can effect meaningful change, both in our personal lives and in our communities. Let's embody the spirit of Dr. Mary McLeod Bethune, honor her legacy, and continue her work, ever striving for equality, justice, and a better world for all. It's now our turn to take the baton and continue the race. Let's do so with courage, determination, and grace, just as Dr. Bethune would have wanted us to.

Greatness is not about where you start, but how you finish. As we embark on this journey of transformation, let's do so with the conviction that we, too, can leave an enduring legacy of love, just like Dr. Mary McLeod Bethune.

7 Affirmations for this Chapter

1. My journey to self-discovery is guided by the wisdom of trailblazing Black icons who came before me.
2. I embrace challenges as opportunities for growth, just as Dr. Bethune did in her pursuit of greatness.
3. I am a leader in my own right, advocating for justice and effecting positive change within my community.
4. I nurture my inner strength and draw upon it to overcome any obstacle that comes my way.
5. Cultural appreciation is a cornerstone of my journey, fostering unity, understanding, and celebration.
6. I am committed to living a life of purpose, leaving a legacy of love and empowerment for future generations.on this journey of transformation, let's do so with the conviction that we, too, can leave an enduring legacy of love, just like Dr. Mary McLeod Bethune.
7. I will willingly share my knowledge with others and lift as I climb.

Here's to our journey to greatness. Now Go Out There and...

BE BETHUNE!

From the cotton fields to Statuary Hall, Congressional
Building Washington DC

Relevant to the Cultural Development of Students and Teachers

Dr. Mary McLeod Bethune

History of

Dr. Mary McLeod Bethune

Why it is Relevant to the Cultural Development of Students and Teachers

"Sometimes I ask myself if I have any other legacy to leave. Truly, my worldly possessions are few. Yet, my experiences have been rich. From them, I have distilled principles and policies in which I believe firmly, for they represent the meaning of my life's work. They are the products of much sweat and sorrow. Perhaps in them, there is something of value. So, as my life draws to a close, I will pass them on to Negroes everywhere in the hope that an old woman's philosophy may give them inspiration. Here, then is my legacy." Excerpt from *The Last Will and Testament of Dr. Mary McLeod Bethune* written for Ebony Magazine 1954.

Dr. Mary McLeod Bethune is one of the most prolific women of the 20th Century. As a sharecropper, Missionary, teacher, administrator, community and civil rights activist, organizer, founder of institutions, program developer, author, columnist, entrepreneur, business advisor, advisor to United States Presidents, peacemaker, fundraiser, motivator, dream builder, woman of God, wife, mother, sister, friend, college founder and president, she accomplished more with her limited resources than many did with access to so much more. Knowing about her and understanding her relevance in the history of this country is a critical part of understanding the very nature of the people who were granted freedom in 1863.

Dr. Mary McLeod Bethune was born in Maysville, SC, on July 10, 1875, to Samuel and Patsy McLeod. She was the 15th of 17 children and the first child of this sharecropping family, born free. She was born into a position of honor and in her words, was seen as "different" right from birth. She looked different from her brothers and sisters and had different tastes and sensitivities. She also had a different kind of spirit and perceived things with a different kind of insight. She was a "giver', born with a deep desire to care for others. It was natural for her to share and when she began to get an education, she did not hesitate to share what she learned. It was the "different" in her that opened the doors for her education at a time when African people in America were not deemed worthy or capable of learning. Mary Jane McLeod took education seriously because, as she stated, "*anything that a person will fight so hard to keep you from getting must be mighty important*". She set a standard of excellence for herself because she knew that she was not just representing herself but her family and her community. She married Albertus Bethune in 1897 and gave birth to her only child, Albert McLeod Bethune, Sr. in February 1899. She continued to work as a missionary and teacher and helped to start mission schools for black children.

In October 1904 after moving to Daytona Beach, Fl., Mary McLeod Bethune started Daytona Normal and Industrial

School for Girls with "$1.50, faith in God, 5 little girls, one little boy (her son Albert) and the ability to make others see her dream. Today that school is Bethune-Cookman University where she was president until 1942 when she appointed her successor. She returned 4 years later as president once more at the age of 71 and a year later appointed Dr. Richard V. Moore. In 2004, Dr. Trudie Reed became the first woman president since Dr. Bethune and has accepted the challenge in the same spirit of faith as her predecessor. .Dr. Mary McLeod Bethune's faith in God was one of the driving forces that moved her to achieve at a level unmatched in her lifetime and seldom since her death. In spite of the obstacles of racism and discrimination Dr. Mary McLeod Bethune left her imprint of excellence on her accomplishments yet her humbleness of spirit is an example of what Faith, Hope, and Love can do in advancing not just a community but a nation.

As educators struggle to teach children filled with low self-esteem and with few examples of excellence outside of athletes and entertainers, the legacy of Dr. Mary McLeod Bethune offers an opportunity to both teacher and student to have a *"teaching moment"*. Far too many teachers with diverse classrooms have limited knowledge of the positive reflections of the children they instruct. The image of Martin Luther King, Jr. has become the poster child of Black history and MLK Day. Too many of the children who see his image have no idea who he is and the sacredness of his humanity. Our history is so much deeper and incredibly wider than the snapshot in time that is Martin Luther King, Jr. or even Malcolm X. The Life and Legacy of Mary McLeod Bethune stretches from South Carolina to Washington, DC; from Daytona Beach, FL to Liberia and England where Lady Astor took note of the strong black woman who believed in world peace; then a blessing from the Pope, in Rome for good measure. Eleanor Roosevelt called her *friend*.

If this black woman from the cotton and tobacco fields of Maysville, SC, with so few resources, could reach the status of Presidential advisor, earn international recognition in 1949 when Haiti presented Dr. Bethune with its Medal of Honor and Merit, and in 1952 Liberia gave her its Star of Africa award then surely OUR CHILDREN, with access to so much more, can achieve even greater. But the children and the ones who teach them MUST believe that they can do it. These children of promise must be taught in a framework that offers them reflections of their greatness with images and examples that look like them. The standards set by Mary McLeod Bethune are as important today as they were when she was alive. Strength of character, respect for power and authority, racial dignity, dedication to one's fellow man or woman, love, faith, hope, and just as importantly a responsibility to the success of our children, are standards for living that hold value even today. Teachers must know enough about the culture of the children they teach to pull out the positive and not the stereo-typical and help children maintain their "zeal" for learning. They must create endless "teaching moments" that engage the mind as well as touch the soul. Children must feel good about learning and understand that it is okay to be smart, read well, and be able to understand and communicate using the King's English. Mary McLeod Bethune did that. What better example for today's youth than one who "performed" spoken word with Langston Hughes and encouraged James Weldon Johnson? Dr. Mary Jane McLeod Bethune laughed often, loved deeply, and was not afraid to stand up for others. Her motto was "not for myself, but for others" and that was how she lived her life. Her creed of excellence will always be relevant, even in the 21st Century.

Dr. Mary McLeod Bethune
Public domain

Support A Movie

Why a movie about Mary McLeod Bethune?

Mary McLeod Bethune was able to come out of one of the darkest periods in American history because of who was holding the lantern, Her parents, Samuel and Patsy McLeod. They were the spark. The story of my great-grandparents is a story of faith, love and the strength to be self-determining. The life of Mary Jane McLeod is what comes from that story. It's almost impossible to tell her true-life story without also talking about Samuel and Patsy McLeod. You see my great-grandfather and my great-grandmother were enslaved in this country, yet they produced one of the greatest American icons that ever lived. Some would say, how is that possible? Well, history doesn't record much about my great-grandparents only of my grandmother, Mary Jane, McLeod Bethune. I find it interesting that so little is mentioned of her roots as it was her parents who gave Mother Dear, as we called her, the foundation upon which she built her life, and her dreams, personality, and natural characteristics were passed through her bloodline, her greatness DNA.

Samuel and Patsy McLeod are the GPS to understanding her ability to press through incredible obstacles of the past and connect her heritage to the legacies she left behind. Would Mother Dear have accomplished so many great feats were it not for the strength of Samuel and Patsy McLeod? You see when Samuel McLeod met Patsy McIntosh, they were enslaved in South Carolina. Patsy was on the McIntosh plantation. And my great-grandfather Samuel was on the McLeod plantation. Yes, that's right. Their last names of course were the names of the plantations upon which they enslaved. In order to tell the story of Mary McLeod Bethune and her lineage, her parents, Samuel and Patsy, and my great-grandparents, who were enslaved in this country have to be a part of that story. Today, we spend a great deal of time and money researching why our communities, the black communities are in crisis. We want to figure out where we went wrong and why we have not made any lasting great progress as a community in over 400 years. Why is it still such a struggle to get and stay ahead of the wave?

It is my belief that we must remember where we come from and who brought us if we're to fix what's broken. The media, our day-to-day encounters with the stereotypical assumptions, and the vast technological environment that we live in, all tell us that black people are generally bad, dysfunctional, and genetically predisposed to lower intellectual achievement more so than others, especially Caucasians. We've spent a great deal of time, ingesting so much negative garbage it is no wonder we're dying mentally and physically at a faster rate than anyone else on the planet. Would my grandmother, Dr. Mary McLeod Bethune have been able to accomplish any of the feats for which history remembers and celebrates her if Samuel and Patsy had not been her parents? Their strength was her strength. They anchored her in faith. They lit the candle that cursed the darkness and they helped her to know who God was. That's why she spent her young educational years studying to be a missionary. It was in her heart and in her spirit, it was her driver. Samuel and Patsy McLeod's love for God and family was the spark that ignited the fire in her soul. Her faith is what kept it burning.

Mary McLeod Bethune was a visionary. God gave her that gift. Today that vision is her legacy. Bethune Cookman University, which was founded in 1904, and the National Council of Negro Women founded in 1935. She merged her school with Cookman Institute in 1923 officially making Bethune-Cookman co-educational. As she grew and developed the college, her state and national influence also grew. Her friendships included the Rockefellers, Thomas A. White, founder of White Sewing Machine Company, Gamble of Proctor and Gamble, and many more who vacationed in the Daytona Beach area. My grandmother became an advisor to four United States presidents. Who would have thought that a little black girl from the back woods of Maysville, South Carolina, where they grow cotton and tobacco would be an advisor to four United States Presidents? Calvin Coolidge, Herbert Hoover, Franklin D. Roosevelt, and Harry Truman. Presidents Coolidge and Hoover appointed her to the National Child Welfare Commission. Under President Roosevelt's administration, she organized the Black Cabinet and was the ONLY female member. This was the case in many, many of her accomplishments, she was the only woman or one of very few. Yet men listened to her. They heard what she had to say. They followed her lead. She understood the value of being a woman. And she cherished being a black woman. She was also Presidential Advisor on Minority Affairs and became Director for the Division of Negro Affairs for the National Youth Administration making her the highest ranking African American civil servant employee in the country. Yes, things were difficult, but she never gave up. She never gave in. And she seldom took no for an answer.

When she started her school, The Daytona Normal and Industrial School, the only land she was allowed to purchase was the garbage dump, Hell's Hole. But she did not let that deter her. Imagine that people could learn in the middle of a garbage dump. She began with $1.50, five little girls and one boy, her son Albert. He would help her throughout the building of this incredible educational institution which is now Bethune-Cookman University. When black people in Daytona Beach and the surrounding area couldn't go to the beach, the world's most famous beach, She didn't protest. She went right down the road to New Smyrna, organized a team of Black people, and purchased three miles of beachfront property They had the river on one side and ocean on the other. They owned the land. This financially astute group of investors sold lots to other black people. This created a recreation area where black people could bring their families, relax, and have fun in the sun without the stress of whether someone was going to arrest them for getting into the ocean. Can you imagine someone saying that you can't get into the ocean without permission from a white person? Wow. What kind of mind comes up with that?

In today's world, we are still given limited space to recognize the beauty and depth of Black people and all that we have accomplished. We seem to be waiting on permission to share our knowledge, to spread the good news. We talk and think about all of the well-known names of Black people only in the month of February. We say Black History 365 but we don't do it. I propose that we share a Black History Fact every day, 365 days a year. We know Martin Luther King Jr., Malcolm X, Sojourner Truth, Ida B. Wells, Frederick Douglas, and Rosa Parks, yet there are so many others. Think about this... Before there was Martin and Malcolm, there was Mary, cutting a path so that they would have a path upon which to walk. She hung out with Langston Hughes and Zora Neale Hurston, W.E.B. Debois, and Carter G. Woodson. She was a Daughter of the Black Revolution with Ida B. Wells and Madame C. J. Walker. Fearless yet a strategist.

But little is known about the full depth of the accomplishments of this great woman. That's the reason that our movie and series are necessary to tell the story. The life of Dr. Mary McLeod Bethune is not monolithic. It is deep and wide and definitely worth telling. You see, the story is about the greatness that lies within ordinary people. When we just obey the call, we don't hesitate when we don't think about it. We just step out on courage. We step out on our faith. We trust in God, which is what Mary McLeod Bethune did. Unceasing favor was granted to her that lasts to this day because I truly believe that Bethune Cookman thrives because of the favor garnered by Mary McLeod Bethune.

So, think about it, invest in the human spirit, who knows it may be a diamond in the rough. Those are the words of Mary McLeod Bethune, encouraging, uplifting, and always forward-thinking a movie on the life of Mary McLeod. Bethune is not just necessary. It's visionary. I believe that it opens doors and begins a new generation of visionaries who are moving forward in spite of the obstacles because once they know that it can be done, they know that they can get it done too.

So, let's move forward. Let's make this movie and a mini-series on the life of Mary McLeod Bethune and all the personalities that crossed her path. Take her life out of darkness into the light of freedom. Share this with your friends. Better yet, share it with Netflix, Disney, Paramount Studios, Tyler Perry,

Oprah, Viola Davis, Shonda Rhimes, and anyone else that you can think of. There is power in the PEOPLE

Dr. Evelyn Bethune
Dr. Mary McLeod Bethune Foundation, Inc
History in the Making Coaching Network, Inc.
Phone: 386-265-3733
E-mail:drevelyn@greatnessdna.com

DrEvelyn is an award-winning author, lecturer, radio program host, and motivational speaker and she is the granddaughter of Dr. Mary McLeod Bethune. One of the goals of Dr. Evelyn Bethune is to train faith leaders on connecting our ancestral history to the strength of our purpose and our faith. "It is essential for our people to KNOW our history and that it did not begin on a plantation as enslaved Africans. "You cannot teach what you don't know. We cannot depend on others to teach and train us to be free" Our DNA has great power, and we must claim our space in a world bent on writing us out of history". Using the legacy of her own grandmother Dr. Mary McLeod Bethune and a family of community servants as examples is a commitment to ensuring that the history of Black ancestry and the great accomplishments throughout the world of Black people will never be forgotten.

Dr. Evelyn is the author of several books, among them is the award-winning Bethune: Out of Darkness into the Light of Freedom which tells the story of her grandmother, Dr, Mary McLeod Bethune from a very personal family perspective. Her book, Call & Response refers to the Black church "Call & Response" of lining hymns and scriptures. She uses the Last Will and Testament of Dr. Mary McLeod Bethune as the Call with the Response of the grands, great-grands, and great-grandchildren. Can You Hear Me Now is a collection of essays and blogs written by Dr. Evelyn for various platforms and covers topics from faith to politics from love to forgiveness with many taking a close introspective look through the eyes of the author. DrEvelyn has also collaborated in several compilations, The Queens Legacy, Choose Purpose over Fear and just recently released, A Mother's Heart just in time for Mother's Day. Her writings continue with a new release expected in September of 2023, entitled, The Bethune Blueprint: Transform Your Life Using Lessons From Dr. Mary McLeod Bethune.

Dr.Evelyn earned the Diana to Deborah Award for Community Services in 2022. She was selected as A Phenomenal Woman in 2015, and one of the Most Influential Women in Business for 2012 and 2014 by the Daytona Beach Business Journal. She was the first African American woman to own a racing team with a car on the NASCAR Track in Daytona Beach. The team was named Racing for Education. She is the CEO of *History in the Making Coaching Network, Inc.*, and a Managing Member of the Dr. Mary McLeod Bethune Foundation, Inc. Dr. Evelyn Bethune introduces her new project, the History in the Making Coaching Network, aimed at helping individuals recognize their inherent greatness and purpose. Drawing on her personal experiences and as the granddaughter of an American icon, Bethune emphasizes the importance of knowing one's worth and not allowing challenging circumstances to hinder personal growth. Through the network's Master Class, Greatness is In Your DNA, individuals can learn to activate their purpose and reach their potential. Bethune's project is a manifestation of her faith and dedication to helping others live their best lives.

MESSAGE from Dr. Evelyn Bethune

I am so excited about my new project, History in the Making Coaching Network, Inc. This new, purpose-filled venture allows me to use the tools God gave me to assist others in knowing that greatness is in our DNA. I am excited about it not just because it puts order to what I was called to do, but because I get to step outside of the box that I have found myself in for the past few years. As the granddaughter of an American Icon, it is often difficult to have my own identity. From childhood that has been a blessing as well as a curse. With my experience in overcoming great adversity as you deal with the consequences of bad choices, bad decisions, or simply trusting the wrong people, History in the Making Coaching Network allows us to provide the tools, training, and resources to help others move into their purpose, choosing purpose over fear.

Never give up and **Know Your Worth** so that you don't allow your past mistakes or even present circumstances/situations to direct your future path. People throw people away, but God never will. He values us even in the midst of our distress. As women, it is critical that we know our worth so that we can reach the heights that God has for us. Walking in our purpose requires that we know the value we bring and not allow the "fleeting moments of insanity" to overtake all that is good and wonderful in our very being. In our Master Class, **Greatness is In Your DNA**, we show you how to connect with the best of your gifts and activate the greatness of your purpose. This is my way of sharing all that God has protected me from and how my faith has enriched my ability to live my best life. BE BETHUNE

Other Accomplishments/Recognitions

- Top 10% of the Class at Bethune Cookman University (College), & Who's Who - 1979
- Listed in Who's Who in American Colleges and Universities - University of Florida1994;
- One of the First African American Women Students at the University of Florida inducted into the University Students' Hall of Fame in 1994;
- Florida Blue Key Honor Society 1993.
- Several recognitions in the United States of America's Congressional Record and state governments.
- Business owner for over 40 years.
- First African American Woman to own a race car in the Rolex at the Daytona International Speedway - #19 Racing for Education

Over the years, Evelyn Bethune has worked with and mentored hundreds of students through high school and college. She has a passion for helping solve problems and bringing a positive end to what can sometimes be difficult situations. Dr. Evelyn Bethune instructs "non-violent" communications, oral and physical (body language), and promotes an environment of consensus. She is at her best serving the public.

I AM A
BLACK
WOMAN

Passing the knowledge

Printed in the USA
CPSIA information can be obtained
at www.ICGtesting.com
LVHW011450271023
761775LV00074B/774